THE PERFECT PIECE

Monologues from Canadian Plays

THE PERFECT PIECE

Monologues from Canadian Plays

Edited by Tony Hammill

Heinemann
Portsmouth, NH

Heinemann
A division of Reed Elsevier Inc.
361 Hanover Street
Portsmouth, NH 03801-3912

Offices and agents throughout the world

Cataloguing in Publication applied for.

Printed in the United States of America on acid-free paper

99 98 97 96 95   DA   1 2 3 4 5 6

This book is dedicated to
playwrights who bring life to
ideas with words and to actors
who bring life to words
with body and soul

        &

to GAY REVELL
who envisioned the book.

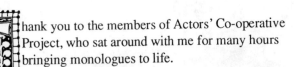

T hank you to the members of Actors' Co-operative Project, who sat around with me for many hours bringing monologues to life.

Bob Bidaman, Anita McGee, Walter Teres, Susan Davie, Jillian Hart, Rachel Lovewell, Benson Simmonds, Bonita Beech. Special thanks to my editorial assistant and actress extraordinaire, Glenda Richards (*second from the left, top row*).

TABLE OF CONTENTS

INTRODUCTION

EAD THE PLAY! Read the play! Read the play. There, I've said it—three times, for that matter, though it can't be said enough. This book is meant primarily for the actor with some time-worn advice. Pick the pieces you think might get you a job and then go read the plays they are taken from. An artistic director knows when an actor understands the character, where he's been, where he's going, what he's doing and why. The only way to discover this is to read the play. Don't sabotage yourself and memorize one page from this book and then "wing it." If Martha Henry says so and Uta Hagen says so then it's most probably right.

There are more than 130 monologues in this book but that is just a sampling of the more than 1,000 Canadian plays available through Playwrights Union of Canada and listed in our free catalogue. You might read a play and find an even better monologue for your needs.

We hope this book will also provide an enticing glimpse into Canadian drama for people who don't generally read plays.

The last 20 years have seen great developments in Canadian theatre, not the least of which was the formation of two small playwright organisations which later merged to form not only a national advocacy body of 300 members but also the largest publisher of Canadian plays. In 1971, the small but hopeful Playwrights Circle was formed by Carol Bolt and Len Peterson, among others, to promote production of Canadian plays on Canadian stages. The next year the group became Playwrights' Co-op to ensure publication of these plays. Growth to national status prompted another name change to Playwrights Canada and official incorporation. Meanwhile, the Guild of Canadian Playwrights was formed in 1977 to protect the authors' rights and fight for their interests expecially regarding contracts with theatres. In 1984 both groups merged to form Playwrights Union of Canada.

From the days of our colourful, cardboard-bound playscripts, to our typewritten paperbacks we have evolved to our state-of-the-art trade paperbacks that are garnering world-wide recognition for our publishing imprint, Playwrights Canada Press. As a pioneer in publishing Canadian plays we like to think we were and still are, an impetus to the many other large and small publishing houses who have decided drama is a worthwhile venture, especially marvelous two-person outfits such as Blizzard Publishing which is devoted entirely to Canadian drama. Bonne chance! We publish six plays annually and have embarked on special projects such as this book not only to showcase the talents of Canadian playwrights but to serve as an aid to players in the theatre.

What is the perfect piece you might ask. In fact, some of the actors who helped on this project, by lifting the pieces off the page, questioned the inclusion of some of the monologues. They are in the book because, while they may not work for one actor, they could well be perfect for another. Hopefully these monologues will not only highlight your strengths but provide an insight into your subtleties as well. There's only so much you can do in two minutes so experiment, choose wisely and shine!

The pieces in the book have been selected from professionally-produced plays written by both past and present members of PUC, as we affectionately call the Union. Like most monologue books, this one consists of a female and a male section but, unlike other books, we have not applied specific age ranges to the pieces but have, instead, put them on a chronological spectrum so actors can wade in and use pieces they are comfortable with. The times assigned are only approximations for your convenience. Your own timing may differ. We did not divide them into dramatic or comedic categories. That is up to you. If it's funny to you or evokes a deep emotion, find the truth in it and trust your innate sensibilities and intelligence to convey your belief in it.

Auditions are, no doubt, the bane of an actor's existence though I do know a few who actually enjoy them. They are, however, a necessary evil in the quest to be seen and be cast. With excellent material, your talent and some homework you'll bring the house down.

Break a leg,
Tony Hamill
Editor

Okay, I admit it! I'm not where I thought I'd be. It's no state secret. I, Daniel Corry, have not achieved all that I wanted to by my thirtieth year. I'd give it to you en français to make it official but so far I've only had two lessons. I mean, look, there are a lot of people who don't make it till later in life. Look at, aaaahh … Oppenheimer! He didn't invent the atom bomb until he was forty one! … Okay, bad example, but you see what I'm driving at? Every time I go home I get these not-so-subtle messages from Mom who leaves these newspapers and magazines open to the career opportunities section. You know the kind of stuff. The first time, I saw them in the living room I thought she was getting ready to paint the ceiling! Then, there's Dad, poor Dad … You know once he compared my life to a broken mirror. Just a bunch of pieces not worth a damn … Well, he was right about the pieces, but dead wrong about it not being worth a damn. At twenty-three I put myself through acting school working in a factory, a sewage treatment plant, and an old folks' home … Glendale Rest … do you have any idea what it's like to sit in a dark room at three o'clock in the morning, holding the hand of an old woman who's dying, alone. Just listening to her breath getting shallower, fainter, watching a life evaporate until it's all gone … Aaaah. Look I've had funny jobs and boring jobs, been a store detective and a waiter, all because I want to be an actor most of all! … Pieces? Yes! But not a broken mirror, a mosaic at least, or a stained-glass window, little pieces making a whole … No, thank you very much for the offer, old boy. But Danny's okay, and Danny will be okay.

2:05

TWO FOR THE SHOW
by Brian Tremblay
Available from Playwrights Union of Canada as a copyscript.

Waiting for the callback.

LADIES

RUBBER DOLLY

by Don Hannah

Two sisters from Newfoundland battle poverty in Toronto's East End. Marie maintains a level of stability while Fern plunges into a world of crime and tragedy.

1:50

MARIE

Hey, member when Donna an me usta drive ya crazy wit em Barbie dolls? We usta go out back past the fields one summer an play Barbie Goes Swimmin? (*laughing*) We take the clothes offa the Barbies an you'd get mad cause we dint have no bathin suits for em. Then we'd throw em in the creek like they uz divers. Jeez, you uz funny. Ya couldn't reach'm an ya's allays such a scardy cat bout gettin wet, so we'd keep tossin em in an makin em swim under waters. Then Donna'd start talking in at funny lil Barbie voice. (*mimicking*) Lookit me, I kin swim, I kin swim.

Oh, she uz so stupid soundin back then fore all at crap wit at guy from the liquor store's wife. I kin still hear her. (*mimicking*) Lookit me, I kin swim, I kin swim, oh help me, Fernie, I'm drownin, I'm drownin. An she'd throw old Barbie in again an you'd cry an scream blue murder. (*laughing*) Then, then the bess part, we'd take em out a the water and shake em round like this (*shaking invisible maracas*) so you'd hear the water inside a em, an we'd sing tha funny song. (*singing*) La Cucarach, la cucaracha. Member?

An when ya heard that water splashin in em ya'd just get crazy. So we'd hold em way up here so ya couldn't reach. (*pausing*) Aw, maybe we uz mean teasin ya like that, Fernie, but Jeezo, ya shoulda seen how funny ya looked. Ya was so funny when ya got mad back then. Jeez youse cute. (*shaking maracas*) La Cucaracha. Jeez.

Available from Playwrights Union of Canada as a copyscript.

DORA: A CASE OF HYSTERIA

by Kim Morrissey

A feminist play about Sigmund Freud and his famous 16-year-old patient.

1:00

DORA

No, YOU don't interrupt. Herr Freud, I loathe you. You are like a fetid lump of cheese; you leave your trail of filth and sex and slime like a great snotty slug, across everything you touch. I hate you. And I hate Papa for leaving me here. I only agreed to come because I wished to be cured, and you only talk about things that have no foundation in fact. My father has spent 32 hundred guilden, and I have come five days a week for an hour a day for the past two months, and yet you have done nothing to relieve my symptoms.

If you were a Physician, and not just a Lecturer on Nervous Diseases at the University, you would give me laudanum to alleviate my pain; if you were a Neurologist, you would try to cure us all of this loathsome disease; if you were a Father you would protect your child from such words as I have heard, and such ... insinuations ...

You disgust me, Herr Freud ... Do you hear? ... You disgust me.

Available from Playwrights Union of Canada as a copyscript.

SEE BOB RUN

by Daniel MacIvor

An emotionally-disturbed young woman reflects on her life of abuse and confusion as she flees the scene where she shot her boyfriend.

2:45

BOB

And I come home. And there he is. There he is. Sittin on a kitchen chair in the living room. I hate that so much. Kitchen chairs are for the kitchen. And the TV is on some stupid kind of movie they put on in the afternoon for people who are scared to go outside. And he starts. "C'mere." "C'mere." But ugly. Ugly like he knows I'm not comin here. I'm goin to have a beer cause I'm hot but there's none. So I go into the bedroom cause I'm gonna listen to some music or somethin but he comes in. He's sayin all this junk but I'm not sayin nothin back cause I don't wanna. And he knocks all my stuff on the floor off the dresser. Like that's gonna make me say somethin but it don't. I got nothin to say just "leave me alone" but I'm sick of sayin that. LEAVE ME ALONE. And he goes outa the room. It's quiet. Shh. Quiet. Good. That's good. Quiet. All of a sudden. First real low. He's playin the guitar. So low I'm not sure if I'm really hearin it or if it's just in my head but then he starts singin. Singin ... "I brought a love, in a cage, to your house, darling, and I let it go ... " Singin that, which I don't want to hear, which I really really don't want to hear. Starts singin it louder. I slam the door. More loud then. Loud like I never thought he could sing that loud. Could anyone ever sing that loud? "I brought a love in a cage to your house darling and I let it go ... " I got my hands over my ears but I can still hear it. I can still hear it like I'm listenin. But I don't wanna. God! Shit! STOP! STOP! And I get up off the floor cause I'm on the floor. I get up off the floor and I go over to the closet. I start pullin stuff out. Diggin through all this stuff. Lookin for it. Lookin. I know it's there. And there it is. The box with the big thick mailman's elastics around it cause the top is broke. I open it up and I'm thinkin about how it was a present from Daddy but he never really gave it to me but it was the one he taught me on and he never took it with him when he left like he wanted me to have it. And there's already bullets in it from long long ages ago. All I'm thinkin is what if it don't work. What if it don't work? That's in my head but not in my body. My body gets up and walks the long way around through the kitchen to the living room. Not even scared. But my head's freakin out. What if it don't work? What if it don't work? And he's still singin. Loud loud loud and fast. I think I'm cryin. Or my head is. I'm standing right in front of him now. I got it pointed at him. Right at his head. And he knows I'm there and he won't open his eyes and he won't stop singin and he won't stop singin that song ... and what if it don't work ... and stop. Stop. Stop! Stop! STOP! STOP ...

And it worked.

———————

Published by Playwrights Canada Press—trade paperback.

SKY

by Connie Gault

*A 16-year-old girl is impregnated by her father then mar-
ried off. She has told her naive young husband that she's
carrying God's child and he believes her. Here she speaks to
a neighbour.*

1:45

BLANCHE

You want to know why Jasper thinks this baby's going to be born
today? I bet you can guess. What kind of baby would you expect on
Christmas day, eh? I lied to him. I saw him walking toward me in
the church the day we were married and he had that look on his face
and I said to myself: not this time. He couldn't take his eyes off me
and I knew before the day was out he'd be—they don't take no for
an answer. You know that, don't you? You know that as well as I do.
But that's where you and me part company. You see, I'm smarter
than you. I didn't give a god-damn what happened to me from that
day on except for that one thing. I wasn't going to let him—I made
up a little story. I said it was God's baby. And he couldn't touch me
because after God, he'd get me dirty. And you know what? He liked
the story. He liked the whole idea. Don't you look at me like that.
You think you don't lie? You do it all the time. Ain't it wonderful
that Harry's back—freeloading on you, drinking till he has to crawl
home every weekend and running out to Anne Flynn's farm every
chance he gets.

And you're so happy to be having another kid, aren't you? Christ,
you're never home. You're always off somewhere, either you're out
here nosing around or you're anyplace else anybody'll have you just
about every hour of the god-damned day so you can get away from
the ones you've got.

I don't need you. I can look after myself. Stop looking at me like
that. I don't need you to feel sorry for me. I'm holy, you know, I'm
blessed among women. Everybody lies, god-damn-it. It makes it

easier, don't it? "We're all praying for you, Blanch... ...'re all
praying for you." Don't you think I prayed? Don'... ...think I said
"God, please don't let him look at me like that... ...make him
stay away? Please make him stop?" I used t... ...there and pretend I
could see through the ceiling to the sky. An... ...I pretend I
could see through the sky to where there v... ...I'd look and
look and all I'd see was nothing. Then I'd... ...
(pausing) So—that's how I know everyt... ...You... ...ly
see through the god-damned ceiling, c... ...it works...
though—lying. For a while.

———

Published by Blizzard Publishing Ltd.—r...

NECK-BREAKING CAR-HOP

by Stewart Lemoine

Sandy is the character referred to in the title. A teen-aged employee of a Regina A&W, she explains the origin of her moniker.

2:35

SANDY

Well it wasn't self-defense exactly, but I was defending something … You know, for the Dub I guess. Okay what it was was, he drives up one day when I'm workin. This guy I mean, this guy in a little blue Toyota, and he just sits there and he doesn't turn on his lights, and that's what you're supposed to do so the car-hops know you haven't been served. I was real busy that day so I guess I walked by him a whole bunch of times and didn't notice him so finally he honks real loud just when I'm right in front of his car and, well I was so surprised I dropped the tray I was carryin and there were two empty root beer mugs on it that got broke.

So I clean those up and then I go and take his order which is only for onion rings and orange pop and I tell him next time he comes to the Dub to turn on his lights like the large print sign says to. I guess I yelled at him but you know when you break those mugs they really get pissed off cause it's real glass eh, and they want people to respect that.

So anyways, I bring him his onion rings and his orange pop, and I'm clampin the tray on his window and he says "Hey Sandy, I'm real sorry," cause you see I'm wearin a name tag on my uniform, and he says "Hey Sandy, I'm real sorry but I want to make it up to you," and I say "Sure, oh sure, how? Just forget it." and he says "Sandy, do you ever do drugs?" and I go "Oh no, well you know, once in a blue moon eh … " and then he throws me this little bag and I'm holdin it there and then I think "Whoa Sandy, what if this has something in it, some kind of Angel Dust or rat poison or like that?" so I say "No thank you for the drugs." and I chuck them onto his tray.

Then I ask him if I could please collect for the onion rings and the orange pop and all he does is try to hand me back the little bag, so I just look at him and go "Noooo." Then he says "Suit yourself Sandy the Car-Hop." and turns on his ignition and starts backin out and Christ, you know what? He's still got his mug on the dash and his tray is still clamped on! So I figure no way after breakin two mugs already am I gonna let him just take off with another one and a tray too, so I run out and grab the tray off, and when he stops to take the Toyota out of reverse, I just reach in and grab him in a headlock with one arm and with my other hand I'm reachin for the mug and that's when I heard it break. His neck I mean, the mug was okay, but there was orange pop flyin every which way and I got some of that on my uniform, and a bit of blood too came out of his nose, but you know, my uniform is brown and orange so it hardly mattered cause the pop went on the orange part and the blood went on the brown part and blood dries brown eh, not red ...

So I got arrested and everything, but I got off because everyone knew I was just trying to get back the mug, and if I really wanted to kill a guy, no way I'd do it at work. But I kept the drugs and I never told anyone about that cause I was afraid I'd have to say I smoked up sometimes and I didn't want my parents to find out.

Available from Playwrights Union of Canada as a copyscript.

STREET LEVEL

by Patricia Ludwick

Cindy, 19, works graveyard in a self-serve gas stop on the outskirts of town to pay for dance classes during the day, She talks to a customer who asks her about herself.

1:30

CINDY

What time is it, anyways. Two fifteen. Between three and four, that's always the longest. Nights it's all self-serve and there's not that many customers anyways. And mostly they just pass you the money, they don't say much 'cause they think you can't hear through the glass. You end up staring at the tail-lights going by ... I get to thinking crazy staff sometimes, you know, daydreams, fantasies, like. Not sex or that, just ... Well, I bring my Walkman to work, eh?—we're not supposed to listen to music but there's nobody around to care, so—don't tell anyone I told you this, it sounds real dumb but ... I play my dance tapes, eh? and I go through my routines in my head. When I close my eyes, I can picture the whole thing, my costume with the feathers and the way my jew'lry sparkles, I'm on this big stage in one of the clubs and it's full of people sitting at little tables with the candles flickering ... and then this spotlight comes on, and the whole audience kind of holds their breath? And then I lift my arms and the music begins, and I start dancing. (*using a set of car keys as a belly-dancer's finger cymbals, demonstrates a flourish or two*) It's better than sex, no, really, it is. It's like—everything you ever wanted to say to people, or do for them, and they know it, they're right there with me. Then I ask one of them to come up and dance with me, and pretty soon they're all dancing, like they've always known how to do it but nobody ever asked them before, and they're all laughing, and I'm right there in the middle of it all. And then I open my eyes and I'm staring at myself in a plate glass window. Hey, promise you won't ever tell anybody about that, eh. I'd never hear the end of it if the manager found out. I know, it's prob'ly not really like that, even in Vegas, but there's gotta be some place I can dance that's not, I dunno, down at Centennial Park on July the First, with people wandering around looking for the chain saw contest. Don'cha think?

Available from Playwrights Union of Canada as a radio copyscript.

 was called to an American film audition, a small part, it was explained—a bank lady. Good! I thought, the executive, that's a step in the right direction ... to be seen finally by the casting directors as efficient, normal, attractive.

When I arrived at the audition it turned out to be a Bag Lady and without even asking me to read, the director looked at me and said "you'll do fine." "But," I suggested, "aren't I too young? Too ... attractive?" "No," he said, "a little makeup and you'll do fine."

Clare Coulter
Toronto, Ontario

RUBBER DOLLY

by Don Hannah

Two sisters from Newfoundland battle poverty in Toronto's East End. Marie maintains a level of stability while Fern plunges into a world of crime and tragedy.

1:40

FERN

So when I runs away that time when I uz fifteen, I come ta Trono and slep in the ravine. Mom thoughts I uz at my sister's, my big sister Marie's, an I tolt Marie I uz livin wit Jean, but really I uz down in the ravine. Jean uz by bess frien back then. I met'r on the train comin up here. When I tole her I gots twelve brudders an sisters, she laugh some hard cause she come from Moncton, dint have no big family.

I never laugh so much's tha summer I come up here on the train. Me an Jean's bess friens right away. We met these guys who uz sailors on the train an we laugh all night long. One a em's called Frank an he uz so smart. He showed me a pitture a himself they took on some island in Europe. He uz real hansome. I uz a lil ascared. Cripes, I uz only fifteen. But he dint know that cause I had on make-up an everthin. He put his arm on me real tight an called me Baby, juss like guys did juss in songs I thought.

It uz romantic out there tween the cars. We uz goin by Quebec er someplace at night ... Maybe it souns cheap, but it weren't cause he uz so nice ta me, an we uz on a train, an there uz moonlight an everthin. Like in a movie? Only better. We almose got caught by a conductor, but my sailor uz holden me real tight an whisperin that he woan let nothin bad happen ta me ever.

I never ever seen'm again, but that sailor uz so nice ta me ... No guys back in New Brunswick'd ever think ta callya Baby.

Available from Playwrights Union of Canada as a copyscript.

THE SHUNNING

by Patrick Friesen

Peter is ostracized from his Mennonite community when he begins to question his faith. A decree by the church forces an estrangement from his wife, and the strain of domestic and community pressures forces Peter deeper into isolation.

2:35

HELEN

the two men asked if they could come in and talk to me.

I must not share my bed with Peter, they said. I would surely be damned if I did. Such matters were, of course, right only between husband and wife and only if they shared the true faith and were submissive to the church, Christ's bride.

this was very hard for me, to stay away from Peter. I loved him. I remembered our wedding, how I had vowed to submit myself to him. but he never pushed for it. he must have known what they told me, but he was so proud. he never asked to enter my bed.

I said maybe we should try the way they said. for a while. and maybe he would find his way to a firm faith again. maybe it would help him settle his doubts.

Peter said nothing.

I dreamed our house burned out. from the outside nothing was wrong. everything looked the same. but, inside, the house was burned out. I couldn't see any furniture, no rugs, nothing, just blackened walls, but no smell of smoke. windows were wide open and a refreshing wind was blowing through. everything was quiet. nothing was moving. there weren't even curtains in the windows. I knew it was our house though I didn't recognize anything. I felt somehow clean. not happy, maybe, but not sad either. clean.

I walked over to a window to look out. the house was beside an ocean. on a cliff all I could see was water ... it's not right for a husband and wife to sleep apart. it feels cold. yet, Peter himself feels cold these days.

how could he move so far from me?

I remember him as a boy. skinny. such a serious young man. asking me to marry him. how could a woman say no? he knew me. understood me. I don't know any others around there who would let me live with my dream.

he didn't stop my dreams. until now ... now, maybe, anything can happen.

and I don't know how things came this far, so fast. nothing will be the same. my chest hurts. my heart ... how could a boy hurt me like this? it makes me look in the mirror ... looking at myself. just me and my reflection. no place to hide. father caught me in front of a window once. the light was right. I was looking at myself, a little girl. licking my fingers and tucking a stray hair in place. he wasn't really angry. just told me sadly that people shouldn't look at themselves like that. it showed pride. "vanity of vanities" he said "all is vanity."

what looks back at me these days seems as real as me ...

if only mother was here ... she would find a way to make everything soft. this hardness, how everything is like stones, is for the men. their world. they know how to live in it. not me.

oh Lord, help me. you are the way, the truth and the light. help me understand. if Peter accepts you, is it so important what other things he thinks? does it matter what we think if our hearts are pure?

I can't hear anything. Lord speak.

yesterday, at supper, our hands accidentally touched. a blue spark crackled ... I want him. I don't want to lose Christ.

Published in "New Works I" by Playwrights Canada Press—trade paperback.

JENNIE'S STORY

by Betty Lambert

Jennie consults a doctor about her inability to become pregnant. She discovers that years before, during an abortion, she was also sterilized. Consent was given by her mother and by the priest who impregnated her. Jennie chooses never to be victimized again. She recalls the priest.

1:35

JENNIE

You came to my bed.
I was 15
A man of God.
And one day you took me to a place.
A place called Ponoka.
And they asked me questions there.
Four people in a room, they asked me questions.
Three men and a woman.
But you swore me to silence, and I said nothing.
And then they wrote you. And then they sent you a letter.
And a paper to sign.
And you took that paper to my ma to sign.
And then you come back, and you said, "Jennie,
they're goingta fix your appendix and when that's
fixed, you can come home. I'll be here you wake up." An' then they
put me to sleep.
And you was, you was there I woke up.

And then you went away again.
And then you come to take me home.
And you told me, Jennie, what we've bin doin' is a moral sin, an'
we must confess to God, and we got to stop.
I got it right then, what happened …
Sometimes I think I can't've got it right …
An' you lied to me …It wasn't no appendix …

I got to go to God through you ...
Only here's where I think what I remember can't be true, Father.
Here's where I think what I think can't be so, Father. When we got
back home, to the rectory I mean, I did my confession and you gave
me penance, and you absolved me. (*pausing*)
Then you came to my bed again.

That can't be true, can it?
That can not be true.
Tell me I don't remember it right, Father, 'cause I'm not too bright!
Even when Harry come courtin' me. Even after that. The week
before you married us. After you'd called the banns twice!

Published by Playwrights Canada Press—trade paperback.

THE QUEEN OF QUEEN STREET

by Maureen Hunter

A young girl meets the aged Bertha Rand, the renowned Winnipeg 'cat lady,' after she has been hospitalized. The play explores Bertha's life, including the poverty, the loneliness and the will to survive.

1:20

ALISON

You take a straight-edged razor and you run it right along here. (*indicating wrist*) It's not pretty, what happens next—not a pretty picture. Your body starts to slip away—it's gravity, and you can't move or catch it, only watch. It takes a lot of energy to watch. Eventually you see it way down there, a poor crumpled-up thing, of no importance. And then you faint. I don't recommend it, especially, but I'll say this much. It beats guzzling Javex. You're surprised. You didn't know I had such talent. But I do. I am the high priestess of my own sacrificial ceremonies! So why am I still here, you ask? I tolerate incompetence.

Here's what the doctor writes in his book. Alison is lacking in effect. In effect! She has ideas of reference, delusions of influence. She shows—volitional defect! I'll tell you what I think of that. It's garbage. There's nothing wrong with me—(*lifting her wrist*)—except my aim. (*dropping the wrist*) There's nothing wrong with me, except ... (*beat; a decision*) I'll tell you what's wrong with me. No guts! Now, why doesn't he just say that, why doesn't he write that in his stupid book? Alison has no guts! Period. Simple! He won't do it, though. Know why? Somebody might understand him.

Available from Playwrights Union of Canada as a copyscript.

CHAIRS AND TABLES

by Rachel Wyatt

The story of a dangerous friendship. Alix has once again arrived to disrupt Susan's life and refresh her memories.

1:00

ALIX

Nice weather for the time of year. You sent for me. Here I am. I was in Mexico City—you haven't changed a bit—same hairstyle, same clothes—and I walked into a bookstore and there it was. Heather's latest. *TRANSITIONS* or whatever it's called. A distress signal if ever I saw one. Your subconscious is sending out distress signals.

My mother sent me a super care package when I was in jail. In Africa. I didn't get to wash my hair properly for three months. I was actually in jail when they arrested me. One of Sam's friends was inside for working against the system. They used me as a messenger. Thought I'd go unnoticed—nice Canadian girl visiting a prisoner. They'd been trailing me ... That hand on my shoulder, Sue. I've never been so scared in my life. The voice, so polite, "Just come along with us, miss, if you please." They were going to lock me up forever.

I had this strong feeling that you needed me. I bribed the guard with a necklace Mother had hidden in the parcel. If I asked Mother to knit me a bullet proof vest, she would, you know. She'd go out and get some steel wool and draw it out into long strands and start knitting it. Even though it made her fingers bleed. She'd knit one for you too if I asked her.

We're still fighting them, Sue. Some of us are. Somehow we've got to make them listen.

Available from Playwrights Union of Canada as a copyscript.

DARK SONG

by Robin Fulford

A woman is sexually assaulted by a man she trusts. The play explores her fear, showing how it affects her relationship to the world and to her lover. Ultimately, she exorcises her horror by revealing her attacker.

2:30

LEE

It's like he's a different person, like part of him has broken loose and is coming out to hurt me. I tell him to get out. I want you to leave me alone. But he closes in and I can smell him. I almost throw up. He puts his hand on my throat and tells me to shut up and do what I'm told or there will be trouble. I'm so afraid he's going to hurt me. He turns me around and pushes me onto the dresser. Then he takes the phone off the hook. I think about breaking away but I don't know what will happen if I do. He tells me to take my clothes off. I beg him not to do anything and he rips my shirt off. I feel so small and cold. The skirt he says. I take it off. See, that wasn't so hard, was it, he says. There's something really strained in him. The phone starts to beep because it's off the hook. His hand comes up my leg and grabs me. I try to move away but he pushes me down on the dresser and kicks my legs apart. I hear him undo his pants. Then he tries to go in. He pushes hard and I must have cried because he grabs me by the hair and tells me to shut my fucking mouth. Then he pushes me down again and takes a bottle of face cream and says, there'll be no problem now, that I'll really like it now, and the bastard shoves it in. He's got me by the hair and pumps and says, start liking it, bitch. I want you to move, I want you to moan the right way. I want to know you like what I got to offer. You asked for it. Then he sticks me so hard that I push the dresser and fall. Then I just start shaking and huddle on the floor. He does his pants up and while he's doing that he's taking these deep breaths as if he can't get enough air. I hope he's going to die.

Then the door clicks. Then the door clicks very quietly, but I hear it. I want to scream for help but I don't know if he's really gone or not. I take these tiny steps over to the bed and sit down and cry. I hold my hands between my legs. I see the phone cord and want to plug it back in. I couldn't touch it because his dirt was on it. I pray he's gone. I take a deep breath and go into the living room. Everything is the same except for me. He's gone. I push a chair under the door handle and put the chain on. I take a big bread knife from the drawer. I sit on the couch shaking and crying. I don't know how long I do that for, then I realize the curtains are open. I close them. I need to hide. Then I go in and turn on the bath. I have to wash him off of me. I can smell his stench on me. I don't want to see my body or touch it. It's not mine right now. I have separated from it. Then the water is hot and it burns and that feels right. I sit in a hot bath with the long bread knife and cry because I've been murdered.

Available from Playwrights Union of Canada as a copyscript.

SACRED HEARTS

by Colleen Curran

*Bridget is witness to an event that may have been a miracle.
Her attempts to keep it to herself because it related to her
hidden past are ruined by the faithful who want to believe
that a miracle has occurred. Gretchen, a local failure, tries
to disprove it with a botched news story.*

1:30

GRETCHEN

Yes, I went to Lourdes. It ruined my trip to France. My cousins and
I rented this car and we were sort of on our way to Nice when my
cousin saw this sign. And she said, "Oh Lourdes is just off this way.
I've always wanted to see Lourdes." Just off this way is two
hundred miles. When we got there they decided that we had to do
this pilgrimage and that involves Masses and vigils and everything.
But I don't like being around all these sad women wearing kerchiefs
and looking fervent and depressed and scared. I don't want to think
about being mortal and sinful and how lucky I am not to have some
terrible disease. You shouldn't force a pilgrimage on anybody ...

I went shopping. But the only thing Lourdes has is souvenir shops.
And I couldn't drive so I couldn't take off with the car. And I
wound up feeling so utterly depressed and guilty because my
cousins wound up having this wonderful, moving religious
experience in this holy place where one of the most incredible
miracles happened and I threw it all away. I've done it again with
the miracle in Westfalia. Some things are just too monumental for
me. But that's me all over the place. I've made a real mess of my
life so far. I'm back living at home, the only one willing to give me
a job is my mother. I'm practically divorced. I just want to get out
of my marriage and stay Catholic, too. It's not that I'm one of those
holy, holy people who go around in a state of grace all the time. And
I'm not someone a miracle happens to. But because one did happen
to somebody in my town, I don't know. It makes me feel I can be a

better person. This miracle makes me realize that being brought up Catholic is important to me. Do you get what I'm saying?

Published by Playwrights Canada Press—trade paperback.

*I hope you don't mind ... I brought in
a few props ...*

SEX TIPS FOR MODERN GIRLS

Peter Eliot Weiss

Three girls recount their diverse and often hilarious sexual experiences.

:50

DOT

Okay, so I know this person, nice person, presentable person, attractive person. A fun guy. I'm picking up signals. He sits next to me. He tells me a few jokes. Suggests movies, a hockey game—the Oilers versus the Canucks. The guy is talking my language, right? So my mind starts asking questions. Is this the start of something? What is it the start of? How much do I like this guy? Can this guy kiss? Is he too cute? If I lay this guy, call him Fred, if I lay Fred, where will it lead? Will I have to quit smoking? Eat sushi? What if Fred falls more in love with me than me with him? What if I fall more in love with him than he with me? What if it ends in divorce? How am I going to support two kids as a single mother? Who will ever want to sleep with me once I've gained forty pounds after two kids? This will never work.

Huh. Some wierdo Fred, thinking I'd let him ruin my life.

Available from Playwrights Union of Canada as a copyscript.

NEW AGE

by Vivienne Laxdal

A hospital room in a maternity ward. Night. A new mother stands by her baby's bassinette watching him sleep.

2:45

MOTHER

(*quietly*) Baby? Baby are you sleeping? I've got some things to tell you baby. Before you wake. Before I forget. Before you're too old to understand.

I know you. You've just been born, but I've known you my whole life. And you know me, too.

You know me from the inside. You know my heart. I gave you my heart. Right at the beginning I gave you my heart. You know my breath. I gave you my air. I gave you my food. I gave you my water. I gave you my mind. It's okay though, you know? You shouldn't feel bad about that. No, not at all.

I'm going to know. I'm going to know what you're feeling. I'm going to know what you're thinking. I'm going to know what you're doing. Like nobody else in the whole wide world. I'm going to have eyes in the back of my head. That's what you're going to give me.

And I'm going to be so proud of you. Every single thing that you do. Even when you fill your pants, I'm going to be the proudest person in the world. My baby. He did this. That's what you're going to give me.

And when you learn, I'm going to learn. I'm going to learn that a kitten feels soft. I'm going to learn that the sky changes colour. That the rug is warm, and the floor is cold. That the water is wet, that bubbles burst, that shoes untie. That's what you're going to give me.

And when you hurt, I'm going to hurt. I'm going to hurt so bad. I'll take it all away from you. I'll take away your stomach cramps.

I'll take away your baby teeth. I'll take away your diaper rash. That's what you're going to give to me.

And when you are scared, I'll be scared. I'll be frightened of the fire engines. I'll be frightened of the barking dogs, the windy trees, the planes in the sky, of being alone. That's what you're going to give to me.

And, when you are happy, we're going to hold hands. We're going to fly right up to the sky. We're going to giggle and laugh and cry and play and yell and shout and dance and sing. That's what you're going to give me.

A few hours ago, I thought I was going to die baby. I thought I was going to die. The pain would wash over me and drag me down to places I've never been before. I thought it would never stop. That I'd never come back. And I wouldn't be able to see your face. I wouldn't be able to hear your cry. I wouldn't be able to feel your small hand grasping my little finger. And then, I knew. That no matter how hard, no matter how long, no matter how painful, that you had to be here. That it had to be you and me. From now on.

So this is it baby. I had to tell you. Before I forgot. I knew you would understand.

I am your mother. You are my child.

Happy Birthday Baby.

Written as a self-contained piece and available from Playwrights Union of Canada.

FOREVER YOURS MARIE-LOU

by Michel Tremblay

Leo is a religious zealot and Marie-Lou a cheap chanteuse, and their marriage feeds on despair and frustration. Their daughter struggles to survive in the midst of their merciless war.

1:25

MANON

We'd been invited to Aunt Marguerite's ... It was during the holidays, I think ... They were all there, Mama's whole family ... There must have been fifty people in the house ... In those days we didn't have a car ... We went by streetcar. You were holding Papa's hand ... I was with Mama ... I'd try to walk like her ... to smile like her ... And keep trying to give her my hand too, but she'd always let go ... It's like she'd suddenly forget she was holding it and she'd let it go ... When we arrived at Aunt Marguerite's they all rushed out to see us ... You know what they're like, Mama's family, real slobberers, always smothering you with kisses ... Then suddenly Grandpa arrived and he swept us both up into his arms, laughing all the time. I was all excited because he was so big and he made me feel so tall. He looked at you and he said,

Why you little bugger, if you don't look just like your mother.

Everyone laughed ... When he turned to me I stopped laughing because I knew what he was going to say. I started fighting to get down because I didn't want him to say it.

And you, Manon, the spitting image of your father.

I could have torn his face off! They talked about it for a long time after ... How I lit into him, scratching and kicking, screaming like a maniac ... When they finally calmed me down I could hear them talking about me, saying what a brat I was, that I didn't have any manners. That I was stupid ... Just like my father!

Little Miss Poison, they called me ... When we got home that night I got the beating of my life ... He was drunk out of his mind and he was yelling,

So you don't want to look like your father, eh? You don't want to look like me!

He knew ...

————

Published by Talon Books—trade paperback. Reprinted with kind permission of J.C. Goodwin and Associates. Translated by John Van Burek and Bill Glassco.

AUDITION PIECE

by Peter Anderson

*A bar. Two close friends, a woman and a man, both in their
30's, sitting at a table. They are slightly drunk, having a
good time. The man is quiet, an absorbed and attentive
listener who obviously enjoys the woman's company.*

1:40

WOMAN

(*to bartender*) Another scotch and soda. (*to man*) How do you like
this dress, sexy isn't it? I'm so sick of this business. Men. I'd like to
puke on the fat slob's face. Who does he think he is? I bust my ass
for years and welfare's after me and all these girls who haven't got a
clue singing crap that died with Peter, Paul and Mary, or should
have, and here I am, they didn't know what to do with me, I was too
hot for them. It's all so demeaning and I'm so horny, Christ. I really
blew it with Rick. I told him I wanted to have a baby and he split.
Why do I always have to do that just when it's going good? The
bum. All he ever wanted to do was drink and go from bar to bar, so
there I am, following him around all night and dragging him into a
yellow cab at 3:00 a.m. just to get him home into the sack with me,
but Jesus, sometimes it don't seem worth the effort, you know? And
then that stupid cat of his driving me bananas. (*to bar*) Where's the
bartender anyway? He got his dink caught in a cocktail shaker or
what? Hey! Scotch and soda, another round. And now welfare's
pissed off at me cause I went to Jamaica with Hank, there's another
weirdo for you. Talk about hang-ups, why do I always pick such
losers? He gets into voodoo and starts thinking I'm a witch or some
crazy shit like that, I don't need it, and his wife still in love with
him after he beat her all the time, God ... so this social worker
wasn't too happy with me after I went to Jamaica, but screw her,
what does she care, she's got a job. And here I am auditioning for
assholes like that, sitting there like he's God almighty, what a pain. I
should've sang one of the new songs I've been working on, if any
of them were finished. I can't seem to finish anything lately.

Whaddya expect? It's all self-indulgent bullshit anyway. Who needs it.

When I went down to the States, people down there, artists anyway, seemed like they had their shit together more, like they didn't screw around and waste time. Here, everybody's so busy trying to act like an artist, being so pretentious and precious and over-intellectualizing everything to death, it makes me sick. I'd rather collect welfare, or get a grant, take the money and run, go somewhere like Jamaica or Tahiti.

Published in "Rattle in the Dash" by Playwrights Canada Press—trade paperback.

JEWEL

by Joan MacLeod

It's Valentine's Day, and Marjorie reminisces aloud about the loss of her husband on the Ocean Ranger and her decision to begin her life anew.

2:15

MARJORIE

Okay, we got our money since then. But I mean this isn't some cheque that just showed up in the mail one day. This is after two years of drawn-out bull shit with lawyers and Louisiana accents. Every time you open the paper or a magazine or letter, more stuff about the Ocean Ranger. What I want, through the whole inquiry, is to narrow it down to one man. But we couldn't even narrow it down to one company. But it's still what I keep wanting, just pare it all down. Leave me one man, up there on the top floor, behind some marble top desk.

I want him to say "Yup, I'm your boy, it was my fault. My fault about the design flaws, the lack of survival suits, my fault about the evacuation procedure and that the lifeboats would've gone down in a lake. I'm your boy. Not that I meant any of it but I sure as hell did screw things up. You think safety is top priority but it gets lost somewhere along the way. You get tested like that and completely fail the test. I screwed up. Big time."

I don't want to cause this man any harm. But I would like to place him aboard a drilling platform, after midnight in February, over a hundred miles from the coast of Newfoundland. An alarm calls this man from sleep and onto a deck that is pitch black and tipped over fifteen degrees and all covered in ice. The wind is screaming. Salt water and snow pelt his face. Everybody is running around and nobody knows what to do. He is in his pajamas and being lowered in a life raft with twenty other men, into a sea of fifty-foot waves.

Then I would reach down and lift that man up from this terrible place just like the hand of God come to save him. Remove him from all that terror and certain death. I place him somewhere warm and dry. Relief here and family. Take his shivering hand inside my own and turn his hand over and over and over. Until he sees it. Palm up and attached and staring straight at him. His hand is the hand of God and he could have gathered them all up. Saved eighty-four men from the North Atlantic. He chose not to.

And I don't care who owns you mister. I don't care if you're ODECO or Mobil Oil, a fed or provincial. My sadness, my husband's death—it was handmade by someone.

Published by Playwrights Canada Press—trade paperback.

THE DONNELLYS,
PART I: STICKS AND STONES

by James Reaney

An Irish family moves to Canada to escape prejudice and violence only to find the new land itself divided and violent.

2:00

JENNIE

Why was I a Donnelly? Because from the courts of Heaven when you're there you will see that however the ladders and sticks and stones caught you and bruised you and smashed you, and the bakers and brewers forced you to work for them for nothing, from the eye of God in which you will someday walk you will see that once, long before you were born, you chose to be a Donnelly and laughed at what it would mean, the proud woman put to milking cows, the genius trotting around with a stallion, the old sword rusted into a turnip knife. You laughed and lay down with your fate like a bride, even the miserable fire of it. So that I am proud to be a Donnelly against all the contempt of the world. I am proud that my mother confirmed my brother in the forest with the fiddle, long before the bishop and the friar could get hold of him, and I wish now I had shared my mother's fate beside her. But oh, still would it have been different. I loved my mother and I nearly saved her even three days before they burnt her with their coal oil.

Because you were tall; you were different and you weren't afraid, that is why they burnt you first with their tongues then with their kerosene.

And there were other times I tried and there was this dream about the time I tried and was to try. And the dream I am going to show you repeats itself to me like a creed I have learned I cannot tell when.

I dream that I've come up to visit the farm, my mother and father are all alone, the boys are all away and I persuade them to leave with me. Before something happens. Good. Because if they leave, then the boys can leave; but if they stay then the boys have to fight for their parents and their work all the time. There's a train we have tickets for and—it stops at the crossing near Andy Keefe's tavern. We have lots of time, except—We spent five minutes catching the dog. And we start walking down the road, when my mother looks back. So we take in the shirts, but the little dog I gave them—

I knew it to be a dream even in the dream because there was still time to catch the train but—there the shirts were on the line again. Mother, come anyhow. We'll wait at the station for the next train. Mother—Father—you've changed your minds about leaving then?

My father and my mother would never leave Biddulph.

Published in "The Donnellys, Part I" by Porcepic Books—trade paperback.

STRAIGHT AHEAD/
BLIND DANCERS

by Charles Tidler

*In the first play, farm-girl Louisa Potter discovers that she
is pregnant. In the second, we meet Louisa two years later
on "the morning after" with a traveling jazz trombonist.
1981 Chalmers Award winner.*

2:10

LOUISA

Yeah ... This weren't the other night I'm talking about, Bone Man.
Don't get your hopes up. This was years ago at a little county fair.
(*pausing*) The last night of the fair, the last couple taking the last
ride on the ferris wheel, and Yulie and me were looking for a hay
stack behind the stables. A bottle of pink sloe gin making a big
bulge in his pants pocket. Ha. We was laughing and drinking and
kissing, having a pretty good time until Yulie started working me
over like a pinball machine. I couldn't move, the big fat pig, but the
first chance I got I clamped my teeth down hard as I could on
Yulie's nose. I had his blower better than a rat's ass in a mousetrap.
He was dancing, screaming to beat the band, his wing-ding naked as
you please by the light of the moon, straight as a shovel handle,
swinging around like a water witcher's stick gone plumb loco.
(*pausing*) Hah. But he let go of me. He didn't want to wrestle no
more. Back home folks call me a bad girl, guess what you'd call a
black sheep you know. But how half-assed wrong can people be?
Oh, I'm a girl all right, but a good girl, a good-time summer girl
who likes a good time, and I do what I have to to get it. I got to
move, I got to keep moving. Damn what people decide to think of
me. And the same goes for you, Mr. Trombone man. And every
other son of a bitch that's ever tried to put a handle on me. Put me
where they want. (*pausing*) Every man I've ever known has tried to
hold me down, has scared me half to death. (*pausing*) My Dad was
the meanest man on earth. I was held down real hard. But my

brother, the baseballer, was the one who ever scared me the most. (*pausing*) One day Chester had no one to catch him, so he takes me out behind the barn and hands me a catcher's mitt. I was ten years old. He tells me to hold the mitt out in front of me, and don't move. Don't move, he says, not one inch, or you'll swallow the damn ball. Now, my big brother was a god to me then ... a seventeen-year-old god in overalls throwing a ninety-mile-an-hour fastball. Zing. Pop. Zing. Pop. Zing. My hand swole up like a small mush melon, but he never hit me once. I never moved. Never swallowed the damn ball. I was to scared to move. Too dumb scared to move. (*pausing*) I ain't no regular bandchick, you see. I don't ball every trombone that comes walking into the Toledo bus station.

Published by Canadian Theatre Review, Spring 1982.

*I realize this headshot's
kinda old. I'm getting new
ones done next week.*

CROWD CONTROL

by Peter Raffo

*Alec and Margie meet again after thirteen years. He wants
to go to the World Cup Finals and she wants to get pregnant; they have only a couple of hours to sort out their
priorities.*

1:25

MARGIE

(*angry*) You see that? You can see nothing! You can have no idea
what it is like! To be a woman at my level, working alongside men?
Listen, I have to justify everything I do, twice. Once because I'm in
the business and once because I'm a woman. Every decision I
make, some asshole wonders whether my hormones were involved
in the process. A guy phones the department I run, he hears my
voice, he asks to speak to my boss, Alec! You can 'see' that? You
see nothing! The jokes? The clubby little snickers behind the pages
of the Business Section? Oh, and the passes, the endless passes.
Drunk and sober, they all make them, sooner or later. There is not
one moving part of the male anatomy that has not, at one time or
another, made its lurch for me. And, of course, when you don't
come through for them, when you make it clear that, just as if you
were an ordinary everyday man, this deal does not come with a roll
in the hay, or on the desk, well … the innuendoes. "Hey, what is
she, anyway? Some kind of a dyke?" So then you have to prove
you're not, so they get what they wanted, anyway. (*pause*) Oh, and I
guess I didn't tell you, did I, Alec? They don't want just sex. They
want the kind of thing mommy bear would never give them, back
home in the den. (*long pause*) That's business, see? I mean, it's
really ridiculous, isn't it? With this body of mine, I should be able to
pick and choose, right? So, why do I always end up with the jerks?

Available from Playwrights Union of Canada as a copyscript.

AUTOMATIC PILOT

by Erika Ritter

A stand-up comic discovers that unhappiness is the source of her creative and comic powers. An expose of modern relationships. Winner, 1980 Chalmers Canadian Play Award.

2:55

CHARLIE

Hi, how is everybody tonight? Come on, it's not a trick question. How about you, sir? How are you? It's all right, sir. I read lips.

Hey, I'm in a great mood tonight. I just got my Mensa card. (*taking a card from her pocket, showing it*) You know what that means? It means I'm insured against ever skipping a period. So ... how do you like my hair? Mr. Doug did it. That's my hairdresser, Mr. Doug. Ever notice what flamboyant names Canadian hairdressers have? Mr. Doug. Mr. Glen. Mr. Garth of North Bay. Mr. Doug told me he was just going to "shape the hair." Notice how they never refer to it as YOUR hair? This is so they can wreck it without either of you feeling personally affected by it.

But I trust Mr. Doug. Implicitly. I mean, he doesn't charge an arm and a leg like those trendy uptown places, where you pay for the decor and the cute little cover-up robe. Mr. Doug works out of an auto body shop. He keeps his costs down that way. Although I notice the Turtle Wax IS doing strange things to my hair. And there was this mix-up one day where a lady came in for a cut and set and wound up getting a ring job. Hey, that's not funny. It's tragic. I suppose you laughed when Ben Hur's mother and sister got leprosy.

Hey, you know, I always wanted to be one of those teensy little girls. You know the kind I mean? The kind of girl whose nickname is Bitsy? The kind of girl I lend a bracelet to, and she wears it as a belt. Helpless. That was always my goal in life. To be helpless. Helpless and sweet and quiet. Like Bitsy. Bitsy never has to talk. She's mastered one simple basic sentence—"How was your day, honey?"—and the world's beating a path to her door. I, meanwhile, am lucky if a guy ventures up my walk to read my meter. See, men just don't come on to big, capable girls—girls who speak English as if it was their native language. Especially when your voice sounds like Full Alert in the London Blitz. I ask a guy if he wants to come to bed, and it sounds like a threat.

Now, Bitsy, has this tiny, feminine, whispering voice, right? Put her on a phone, man, and she gets results. (*imitating*) "Hello? Oh, hi, Brad. Dinner? No thanks. I just ate half a soda biscuit and I couldn't touch another thing."

And when Bitsy goes shopping for clothes, the clerks always advise her to try the Petite Section, right? The Petite Section. It even sounds elegant, doesn't it? So what do they call the large section? You guessed it. The Large Section. And I so much as even try walking into the Petite Section and they throw a cordon around the entire department and get on the bullhorns—(*imitating*) "Attention all staff. Large person attempting entry. Large person attempting entry." Then they send some little Munchkin over to reason with me, right? (*imitating*) "Listen, honey, nothing personal, but you're built like a Maytag, all right?"

You notice how tiny all the clerks are in the Petite Section? The manager of the department wears a point-zero-six dress. I'm not kidding. And when I won't go quietly, the entire staff rushes to the barricades. It looks like a convention of jockeys. They all swarm around my kneecaps chanting—"Follow the yellow brick road. Follow the yellow brick road … "

Hey, you've been a great audience. Thank you and good night!

Published by Playwrights Canada Press—trade paperback.

PEACHES AND CREAM

by Keith Dorland

His marketplace is the food industry, her's is the sex trade.
They struggle to discern the true price of their commodities.

2:30

KATE

It was my first train-ride down to London. I was very nervous and excited. Watching all the countryside go by—country I'd never seen before—and it was a bright sunny day. I'd left my parents, I'd left my job, I'd left my boyfriends who said to me "Don't go down there, luv, you'll only finish up walkin' the streets." "Well," I said, "if I stay here I'll finish up walkin' the streets behind a pram." No way! I was free. I could do anything I wanted. It was like rushing headlong straight to Heaven—everything in the future.

Oh God, I was scared and I loved it. I only thought about the good things that could happen. I'd take my Drama course and be discovered at the big end-of-term production in the role of Juliet. I mean it happened to other girls every year. Why not me? Or I'd find a job in an acting agency where I could meet famous people and be discovered for my personality and bone-structure as the perfect Juliet. "I've trained at R.A.D.A." I'd tell them and the deal was clinched. (*sadly*) It was always Juliet because I believe in her. I really do.

(*deep breath*) Suddenly … This older man sitting opposite me started to talk. He asked me about myself, looked me over, took me into the bar for a drink, bought me lunch, paid me all kinds of professional compliments—fantastic! It was the first time I had ever been chatted up by a total stranger who wasn't drunk or disgusting in some way. In fact, quite distinguished and by all appearances very well-heeled. I could tell he had something he wanted to offer. I was curious to know what it was. And cautious. But he was an older man, twice my age at least, and that lulled me into his confidence. He talked about the club and eventually said there was a vacancy there, and if I was interested all I needed to do was get in touch. He gave me his card—yes, it was authentic—and told me that if I decided to alter my career plans ever so slightly I could give him a call the next week. After all, he was in show business just like I wanted to be. (*beat*) A job! In one of the biggest 'Entertainment' organizations in the world at the tip of my fingers! And all because he'd looked me over and liked what he saw. And he didn't even want anything in return. I was in Harold-Robbins-Land: diamonds, furs, dry martinis with olives, deep-pile carpets and the rattle of dice. Of course I knew it was just the memberships office in the City, and the rest was all inter-woven from my imagination. But still, it was the first time that my good looks had ever really got me anywhere useful. My first taste of power.

Available from Playwrights Union of Canada as a copyscript.

GOODNIGHT DESDEMONA (GOOD MORNING JULIET)

by Ann-Marie MacDonald

Constance Ledbelly, a lecturer in Renaissance drama, is deciphering a coded manuscript which she believes is a lost source for both OTHELLO and ROMEO and JULIET when she suddenly finds herself in the thick of the two plays turning them from tragedy to comedy.

1:55

CONSTANCE

Omigod!
Oh Constance, don't be scared, it's just a play,
and Desdemona will look after you.
Desdemona! I am verging on
the greatest academic breakthrough of
the twentieth century!
I merely must determine authorship.
But have I permanently changed the text?
—You're floundering in the waters of a flood;
the Mona Lisa and a babe float by.
Which one of these two treasures do you save?
I've saved the baby, and let the Mona drown—
Or did the Author know that I'd be coming here,
and leave a part for me to play? How am I cast?
As cast-away to start, but what's my role?
I entered, deus ex machina,
and Desdemona will not die,
because I dropped in from the sky ...
Does that make this a comedy?
And does it prove my thesis true?
In that case, I've preempted the Wise Fool!
He must be here somewhere—I'll track him down
and reinstate him in the text,
and then I'll know who wrote this travesty,

since every scholar worth her salt agrees,
the Fool, is the mouthpiece of the Author!
It's all so strange ... What's even stranger though—
(*counting the beats of her speech by tapping each of the five
fingers of one hand onto the palm of the other, in time with
her words*)
I speak in blank verse like the characters:
unrhymed iambical pentameter.
It seems to come quite nat'rally to me.
I feel so eloquent and ... (*making up the missing
beats*) eloquent.
My god. Perhaps I'm on an acid trip.
What if some heartless student spiked my beer?!
(*stops counting*) Nonsense. This is my head, this is my
pen, this is 'Othello,' Act III Scene iii.
                              Desdemon, I obey!

———————

Published by Coach House Press—trade paperback.

LOVE AND ANGER

by George F. Walker

*Feisty Petie Maxwell, an ex-ritzy lawyer reduced to the
lower echelons by a stroke, and his cohorts vent their anger
and frustration at the big city and its system of power that
leaves them feeling impotent and isolated. They kidnap the
publisher of a red-neck tabloid and put him on trial.*

2:15

SARAH

Big tractor trailers. Hundreds of them. All painted white. Everything
white. White tires. Hundreds of big white tractor trailers thundering
down the highways. Looking for adventure. Looking for a place to
take over. Surround. A small town, surrounded by tractor trailers, is
every small town's worst nightmare. And these guys know it. The
guys who drive these things. Big beefy white guys who bought
these tractor trailers and painted them white. Sold their houses to
buy them, sold their Harley-Davidsons and their kids' roller skates,
made their wives become prostitutes and cashed their baby bonus
cheques, so they could buy their tractor trailers and form a club. A
club that was big and fast and white and thunders down any
highway to any destination and takes over. Big beefy mean white
guys who hate little people. And little cars. But mostly they hate
black people, and brown people and yellow people. So they
surround a town and they take it over and they become the power.
They're indestructible. They're armour-plated. They're full of hate.
And now they've got a headquarters. A centre of operations. First
thing they do is kill everyone who isn't beefy or white. Kill all the
skinny people. And the two black people in town. And the old guy
who owns the Chinese restaurant. Kill them openly. Kill them
without fear. Because they're in control. They're free to be
themselves. Free to be the one thing that's been hidden all these
years. The big beefy mean white guys full of hate. Because some of
them, most of them, aren't really big, don't look big, only have the
big guy *inside* them. The big beefy guy inside them has been talking

to them for years. Telling them to let him out. To do his thing. First get me a machine he says. A big thundering machine, an operations base, a mobile base, a tractor trailer. Get it rollin'. Get some respect. Join up with others. Declare ourselves. Then get a permanent home ... So they did. They got a town. They got it surrounded. And word gets out. Soon it starts to spread. Thousands of white tractor trailers banding together. Taking over towns. Killing little people, brown people, everyone who isn't beefy and white. It's a movement. It's happening everywhere. It's out in the open. It's an accepted thing. It's the way it is. We're surrounded. It's our turn to die ...

Published by Coach House Press—trade paperback.

I enclose an example of how the auditionee is often as nervous as the auditioner. What it doesn't tell is how I later became friends with the whole Fletcher family (including the dog).

In 1968 I met and auditioned for the late Alan Fletcher at his apartment in New York. Alan was, at that time, Artistic Director of the Seattle Rep. There was one member of his family present—Hamlet—a Dachshund. Alan apologized for auditioning me in his apartment, took Hamlet into the dining room and closed the glass doors.

Alan was a shy man and so was I. We mumbled a few niceties and I got on with it. I started with Cornelius' long speech from Thornton Wilder's THE MATCHMAKER. The piece fit me like a glove and I knew he liked it. My second piece was from HAMLET. I began to speak: "O what a rogue ..." There were immediate objections from the canine Hamlet. He barked, he howled, he whined. He scratched at the door.

I tried to bull my way through it, but Alan stopped me and put Hamlet in a bedroom down the hall. He returned, closed the doors and mumbled an apology. Alan was beet red and embarrassed. I continued with the speech but the critic in the bedroom would have none of it. He howled even louder. I flung open the glass doors and bellowed in the direction of the bedroom: "Remorseless, treacherous, lecherous, kindless villain! O, vengeance!" The howling stopped. There was a long silence. I turned to Alan and we both broke up.

I didn't finish the speech. I did get the job. I never played Shakespeare for Alan.

Les Carlson
Burnaby, B.C.

THE REZ SISTERS

by Tomson Highway

Seven women on a Manitoulin Island Indian reserve (the 'rez') decide to travel to Toronto to compete in the world's biggest bingo tournament. Winner—Dora Mavor Moore and Chalmers Awards.

1:10

ANNIE

When I go to the BIGGEST BINGO IN THE WORLD, in Toronto, I will win. For sure, I will win. If they shout the B 14 at the end, for sure I will win. The B 14 is my lucky number after all. Then I will take all my money and I will go to every record store in Toronto. I will buy every single one of Patsy Cline's records, especially the one that goes (*singing*) "I go a-walking, after midnight," oh I go crazy every time I hear that one. Then I will buy a huge record player, the biggest one in the whole world. And then I will go to all the taverns and all the night clubs in Toronto and listen to the live bands while I drink beer quietly—not noisy and crazy like here—I will bring my daughter Ellen and her white guy from Sudbury and we will sit together. Maybe I will call Fritz the Katz and he will take me out. Maybe he will hire me as one of his singers and I can (*singing*) "Oooh," in the background while my feet go (*shuffling her feet from side to side*) while Fritz the Katz is singing and the lights are flashing and the people are drinking beer and smoking cigarettes and dancing. Ohhh, I could dance all night with that Fritz the Katz. When I win, when I win THE BIGGEST BINGO IN THE WORLD!

Published by Fifth House—trade paperback.

IN THE CARDS

by Caroline Russell-King

*Rivka is a reluctant psychic who forsees her marriage to
her childhood sweetheart at age five, shadows him for years
only to abandon him at the altar when she sees a vision of
him in bed with another woman—the woman he ultimately
marries. But of course their paths still cross many times.*

                                                            1:50

RIVKA

I know what some of you are thinking. Is she the psychic? She
doesn't look like a psychic. Surprise! I wasn't born one though. My
childhood was hell. My mother was psychic. The only good thing
was she was the only mother on the block who never asked me
where I was going, who I was seeing or what time I'd be home.
They say mothers have eyes in the back of their heads. My mother's
eyes used to be in the back of my head, on the inside. Most mothers
read romance novels for fun—my mother read the neighbour's
minds. She used to spank me for things I was going to do. When I
was seven, I got grounded for six weeks for something she said I
was going to do in the back seat of a bus when I was sixteen. Most
kids get punished for things they said, I got punished for things I
thought. She threatened to wash my brain out with soap. I'd be
terrified she'd do it one day and bubbles would come out of my ears
at school.

Anyway, my life changed when my friend Daisy and I found a
package of cigarettes on the street, and we decided to climb a tree
and smoked them all. I got dizzy, fell out of the tree—that's when I
learned smoking is hazardous to your health. Daisy got really scared
because I'd hit my head and was unconscious and so she ran to tell
my mum, which was redundant because she already knew. I wasn't
out for very long, but when I came round I found I had the curse
too. No, not that. That didn't happen until I was thirteen. The
psychic curse. At age five, I got even with my mother. We never

really discussed it, but she knew. All I had to do was gasp, or giggle at the appropriate time and watch her cringe. Growing up I found out all sorts of things a child shouldn't know. My mother lusted after Frank, our grocer. My dad fiddled his books, my aunt drank, the minister wore women's underwear. Life isn't pretty when you're psychic, but it sure is colourful.

————

Available from Playwrights Union of Canada as a copyscript.

THE REZ SISTERS

by Tomson Highway

*Seven women on a Manitoulin Island Indian reserve (the
'rez') decide to travel to Toronto to compete in the world's
biggest bingo tournament. Winner—Dora Mavor Moore
and Chalmers Awards.*

1:35

EMILY

Fuckin' right. Me and the Rez Sisters, okay? Cruisin' down the coast
highway one night. Hum of the engine between my thighs. Rose. That's
Rosabella Baez, leader of the pack. We were real close, me and her.
She was always thinkin' real deep. And talkin' about bein' a woman.
An Indian woman. And suicide. And alcohol and despair and how
fuckin' hard it is to be an Indian in this country. No goddamn future for
them, she'd say. And why, why, why? Always carryin' on like that.
Chris'sakes. She was pretty heavy into the drugs. Guess we all were.
We had a fight. Cruisin' down the coast highway that night. Rose in the
middle. Me and Pussy Commanda off to the side. Big 18-wheeler come
along real fast and me and Pussy Commanda get out of the way. But
not Rose. She stayed in the middle. Went head-on into that truck like a
fly splat against a windshield. I swear to this day I can still feel the
spray of her blood against my neck. I drove on. Straight into daylight.
Never looked back. Had enough gas money on me to take me far as
Salt Lake City. Pawned my bike off and bought me a bus ticket back to
Wasy. When I got to Chicago, that's when I got up the nerve to wash
my lover's dried blood from off my neck. I loved that woman, I loved
her like no man's ever loved a woman. But she's gone. I never wanna
go back to San Francisco. No way, man.

Published by Fifth House—trade paperback.

MOO

by Sally Clark

When the feisty and rebellious Moragh (Moo) meets the intriguing Harry, she decides nothing will ever separate them ... and Harry has been running ever since. An unconventional comedy of love and obsession. Moo has been committed to an institution by Harry and is now in a straightjacket.

1:20

MOO

I suppose, these days, it's all in one's credibility. If you are short, you have less credibility than a tall person. If you are a woman, you have less credibility than a man. If you are short, a woman and wearing a straitjacket—well, forget it, you have no credibility at all. I go to the mirror and I stand and look at myself wearing this stupid get-up and I think—"Can I believe this woman?" And the answer is of course, "No." In theory, if I did have sisters and family, they should eventually start looking for me. I don't see anyone except Harry and then, only once a week. Harry, the man I love to hate. I look forward to his visits. For the week, I rage against him; I beat myself against padded walls. I plot and plan all the nasty things I'm going to say to him. Yet, when he shows up, I'm so bloody grateful it's ridiculous. I'm even starting to believe he's my brother. The thing I can't fathom is, if Harry isn't my brother, why is he doing this to me? That's what doesn't make sense. That's what makes me think I must be crazy. Then, it all clicks neatly into place. It all makes sense, then, I'm getting very tired again. I don't know whether it's drugs, bad food or just fatigue, but I sleep all day. I wake up for meals, read the odd book. But mainly I sleep. And await rescue.

Published by Playwrights Canada Press—trade paperback.

COCKTAILS AT PAM'S

by Stewart Lemoine

Estelle, a guest at the eponymous function, discovers that all of the canapés contain an ingredient which is abhorrent to her. A divorcée from Connecticut, Estelle has until this moment been a completely affable party-goer.

2:00

ESTELLE

(*breathing deeply and slowly*) Do I ... not like ... green pepper? Well no, in fact I hate it. Actually, do you want to know what I really hate? I hate the fact that although I despise green pepper, everyone else alive seems to love it. I mean, it really doesn't bother me so much that I don't like the taste, because the reasons for that are certainly either scientific or medical. No, what bothers me is that everyone else likes it and because they do, it is so much in evidence. On pizza, in salads ... The other night I found some in stroganoff! ... yuck ...

And a myth has sprung up you know. People have said to me, "Well if you don't like it, just pick it out." But that's so stupid. Just because you pick it out that doesn't mean the flavour's going to go away. Green pepper doesn't work like that. It is insidious and pervasive, like noxious fumes that kill you and your family while you sleep. Jesus, the way some people talk, you'd think it was parsley! I've even seen, yes it's true, green pepper that has been sliced cross-wise to form a sort of shamrock-shaped ring that then gets tossed onto an unsuspecting casserole. That's supposed to be decorative? Do you believe it? Nothing like adding a garnish to make the bile really rise up in the throats of your dinner guests!

Look, I know you all probably like green pepper and so you think I'm over-reacting. But what I'm really trying to say is that acceptance of these foodstuffs can never be taken for granted. You can't assume it. It's not a given. No. This is something that has caused me a lot of unhappiness and I just don't want to go through that anymore.

(*after a pause, rather tentatively*) I do like red pepper though. I want you all to know that. Do you think that's strange? Well it isn't! It isn't strange at all! They aren't the same, no matter what people try to tell you. They aren't! It's like butter and margarine. Did you know there are people in the world who think butter and margarine taste exactly the same? My husband was one of them. You're probably all just like him! Well ... well ... Well, it's obvious that some people's taste is all in their homes!!

Available from Playwrights Union of Canada as a copyscript.

HOW COULD YOU MRS. DICK?

by Douglas Rodger

A dramatic examination of Hamilton's legendary "Torso Murder" case and the character of the notorious Evelyn Dick. A cross between a whodunit and courtroom drama.

2:15

EVELYN

I can direct you from here. Turn around. I was driving, John was sitting on my right and Bill Bohozuk was in the back seat alone. Straight ahead, here is where the drinking started. Stop here. This is where the bottles were thrown out. They were thrown out of the right side of the car, they will be over here.

School kids have probably found them and turned them in for a few pennies. Drive straight ahead. Stop. This is where we got stuck. Drive on. Turn right. Here is about where John started to get drunk. Both John and Bill had been drinking while we were driving, but I was only drinking ginger ale. Drive on. Turn left. Turn right. At this point John was worrying about being late for work. He had to be back on the job somewhere around four o'clock, and he wanted to turn north towards Hamilton. I saw Bill in the rearview mirror, he was waving his hand like in a 'go ahead motion.' Bohozuk said, "This is a shortcut back to the city John." Turn right here. This road was a mess, mud and water. The windshield wiper was going, we had an awful job keeping the road. When we turned this corner, John got mad and he said, "I can see it all now, it's a plan. Tomorrow I am going to the lawyer to start divorce proceedings and name you as correspondent and instead of you being a big shot you will be the laughing stock of the men down at the plant."

The argument got hotter, until we came to a spot where there were double telegraph poles. This is it right here. Stop. This is where Bohozuk shot John in the neck. (*placing her finger on the back of her neck*) He shot John in the neck and blood spurted out of the right eye. And the blood splashed all over me. He shot him again

- 68 -

right there, through the head. (*placing her finger just about the same spot*) I was choking. The car was full, filled with gunpowder smoke and I was covered with blood. I stopped the car and got out the door and I got sick. I tried to clean the blood off me. Bohozuk got out the right hand door and pulled the blanket from the seat and wrapped it over John's head. John groaned so Bill said "I'll finish him off" and shot him in the chest.

I am not lying, I am telling the truth, and I am not going to be left holding the bag for anybody. Why should I take the rap for someone else?

He drove to the garage at Carrick Street and John Dick's body was placed in the garage by Bohozuk. Then we drove up town to the Royal Connaught Hotel where I let him off. Then I drove back home, stopping at a drug store to buy some 'It' cleaning fluid. I tried to clean some blood off my blouse and my stockings. Then I drove back into the lane to clean some blood off the car. I wanted to get the car into the garage but I couldn't. I took the blanket home and washed it. (*yawning*) Say could we stop at the Majestic Restaurant for supper. I'd kill for a chicken dinner.

———

Available from Playwrights Canada Press as a trade paperback.

I AM YOURS

by Judith Thompson

Dee is a woman incapable of loving, who wreaks havoc on her own life and the lives of the two men she is involved with. She becomes pregnant by one of them and an obsessive struggle to determine the fate of the baby ensues. Mercy is her sister.

3:00

MERCY

You do so remember, you do so, you say you don't, you're lying cause I was there, I was there and you were there: twenty below, twenty below zero running to catch the school bus, all my books fall in the snow, I gotta pick them up, so I miss the bus, have to hitch. Stick my thumb out, this guy pulls over, old English guy in an old blue car, I get in, his name's Raymond, Raymond Brisson, he gives me a smoke, we get talking and like he's really intelligent, he's read *LORD OF THE RINGS*, three times, and like, I'm thinking, this guy could be my boyfriend!! Like none of the other guys at school would even look at me, but this guy, Raymond, he sees, see? He sees what I always knew ... that there's something ... like a star in me, something, like if they really knew me, even the ... truly great would love me ... cause I got—something ...

So we park at the school, bell goes off, "Oh my God, I gotta go," he looks at me, goes, "You know, you might be quite pretty if you lost some of that poundage" ... He said that. He actually ... believed me to be ... lovely. Lovely.

Not like you you Fucker Daddy. I heard you, I saw you giving her that locket 'for my favourite daughter, Deirdre'—that heart with the ICH BIN DEIN engraved. What does that mean, anyway, eh? What the hell does that mean?

So he leans over, his eyes going yellow and he kisses me, put his ... tongue right in my mouth ... like an egg cracking open in my belly pouring out all this like ... honey everywhere, God, I wanted to kiss

- 70 -

him again and again. Shit the bell, "I really gotta go, but, but, I think I'll hitchhike tomorrow" then I see you guys, leaning up against the wall, having your smoke before class, and I walk by you, almost past you, don't want to be late, when "You dropped something." I feel my face turning red; like Christ, what if something dropped from my body or something but I keep going anyway.

"Hey whoredog, we said you dropped something."

Oh my no, that word, no, my heart's falling through my chest, shit, they saw they saw your tongue in my mouth, and my underpants, they know, they know, they're all—shit I can't move, I can't move cause I know I know that they know that they know that I'm a "Hey whoredog! Ya gonna do for us what ya did for that old man?"

I can't cry, no please God don't let me, I shut my eyes, waiting, just waiting for them to go in, I still can't move, I'm just standing there why can't I move when Owwww! Something hit me in the eye. What the Oww!! Owww! Stop it what ... What—pennies! They're throwing ... pennies at me. I don't get it, like what should I do? Nobody—told me—how to act how come God, oww please, how could anyone have so much pennies, and why are they throwing them at me, what did I oww oh no, oh no this is so bad please, Mummy ... when poof I know what to do, I know. So I just bend over, I bend over and I ... pick up their pennies one by one, all hot and greasy, I pick em up—they're still hitting my back, till my fists ... are stuffed, stuffed and I stand up and I walk right to em with my fists out like this (*demonstrating*) right up to em and I go I say, "Here, here's your pennies back." Then they're gone, and I'm standing there ... so when I see you, you know, even though it's twenty years later, it's today, you know? It's now like no time's passed, all now and I still can't look at a penny, I can't, cause it makes me know, you see, it makes me know that I ...am a sick, disgusting whore for letting a guy's tongue in my mouth and especially, especially for letting that ... honey pour that ... feeling ... that I certainly never ... ever ... had ... again.

Published by Coach House Press—trade paperback.

Oh, yes! I took three years of modern and two years of tap.

HOOKING FOR PARADISE

by Sharon Stearns

Set in a Moose Jaw brothel in 1912 the play explores the power struggle between men and women, looking at one woman's attempt to create a matriarchy in a traditionally male-dominated society.

1:15

SPARERIBS

All right. Say you spot this man walkin' into a saloon or a café, right? First thing you do is you look at his eyes 'cause that's where you can tell if he's hungry or not. And you make him look right back into your eyes where the message is ringin' loud and clear. Then you slowly let your eyes travel up an' down his body. Mmmm … like you're checkin' him out real good. Let him know that your hips is into some business. Then you look away cause if he' hot he's gonna want to do a little chasin' and you don't wanna spoil his fun. But you keep thinkin' about how soft you're gonna feel and how sweet you're gonna taste so it spreads a warm glow all over your face. Like you want it so bad you can hardly wait an' he's the only one who can do it. The only one who can make you the way you wanna be made. He'll pick up the scent an' be crawlin' all over you in no time. That's when you gotta start thinkin' about the practical things but you never let him know you're doin' it. Things like how many times he's good for and how much you think you can take him for an' whether or not he might have the clap. And before you know it, you're down on the bed and … and it's … over and … it's never as good as you both dreamed and you try some more and you want that moment to be … like nothin' ordinary. And then … then it's gone. But that don't matter cause it was so much fun gettin' there. An' there's always another one waitin' around somewhere that may be the one. The one that's just like your dream.

Available from Playwrights Union of Canada as a copyscript.

CLAWS

by Lezley Havard

The family cat, left to freeze in the snow, symbolizes the chill that pervades a modern marriage. Both husband and wife feel victimized and seek retribution.

3:30

PAULA

You know, I'm trying to be fair, I am trying very hard to see things from your point of view, but I really cannot accept that the death of Puss is such a tragedy to cause a traumatic reaction. I'm sorry but I cannot accept that. You are, to coin a phrase, 'over-reacting'.

Yes, that's what you're doing, over-reacting. I'll be honest with you, to tell the truth, I did not care for that cat at all. Oh I didn't actively dislike it. I just did not care for it. It's not as if it were my cat. I didn't grow up with it as you did. It only became a part of my life when your mother died. I think I treated it extremely well considering it left hair all over the furniture, considering its favourite sleeping place was *my* pillow, considering it was not the cleanest cat in the world and had a nasty habit of taking its food out of the bowl and carrying it around the house, chewing it up and then regurgitating it onto the living room rug. Considering it clawed the furniture, ran up the curtains and constantly knocked over the ornaments so that we have scarcely a wedding gift left ... and not to put too fine a point on the subject it had incredibly bad aim when it came to its kitty litter. Considering these things and the fact that it SMELT, smelt like a dirty old bag of laundry and that it vomited inside the linen closet, shit in the toybox and in general might be described as a WALKING DISASTER.

I think I treated it extremely well. The final straw came however when I discovered that the baby ... our child ... was asthmatic; that he did in fact have increased difficulty breathing whenever Puss was about. I tried to keep them apart but having turfed Puss out of the crib twice in the same morning, the baby almost choking to death, it was apparent that something was going to have to be done. So you see, looking at it from that point of view, it is perhaps a blessing that nature took the matter out of our hands and delivered Puss into the next world in her own time.

Have you listened to a word I've said? (*pausing*)

I didn't tell you the truth just now, I lied. I didn't just 'not care' for that cat. I hated it. It was an evil-smelling, repulsive animal. Every time it came near me I felt sick. It wasn't the baby who couldn't breath, it was me and not because I'm asthmatic but because the mere sight of that ... thing sidling around behind the furniture made me nauseous. When you went to work every morning the first thing I did was to kick it out of the house. I let it in for five minutes before you were due home and not a moment before. Come rain, snow, fog or thunder, I never let it in. It used to sit on the windowsill, its ugly, old face pressed to the pane howling hour upon hour. I thought I would go crazy. I would draw the curtain and turn the radio on loud ... But every now and then I'd forget and turn the radio down or open the curtain and there he'd be ... Oh God how I hated him ... when I first met you one of the things that drew me towards you was your love for animals. If I'd only known. I thought it was so sweet to see a grown man going all soft and silly over a kitten. It's strange, when you think of it, I'm quite a gentle person by nature. I don't usually feel aggression ... but when it came to that cat ... every muscle in my body would go taut with rage. He was there, tonight before you came home, in his usual place, drooling at the window, nose and eyes running, congealing and freezing to his fur. I watched him as he howled and scratched to come in. I could see he was dying and I was glad. 'Just a little while longer' I kept telling myself, 'you only have to stand it a little while longer, a few more hours out there and it will be all over, no more Puss, no more hair and smell, no more saliva-drenched cushions, no more meeow, meeow, meeow ... '

What is it? What is it, eh? What is it you want to hear? I told you I hated him, isn't that enough? I said I'm glad he was dying, what more? You think it's all my fault don't you, DON'T YOU? You think he died just because I wouldn't let him in DON'T YOU, isn't that it? Isn't that what you want to hear ... ALL RIGHT, ALL RIGHT IT WAS MY FAULT. HE DIED BECAUSE I LEFT HIM OUTSIDE TO FREEZE TO DEATH.

HE DIED BECAUSE I WOULDN'T LET HIM IN. YES, YES, I
KILLED HIM. I KILLED HIM. I KILLED HIM.

———

*Published in "Women Write for Theatre, Vol. 4" by Playwrights Canada
Press—trade paperback.*

FEVER DREAM

by Anna Fuerstenberg

A gritty look at the lives of five strippers and their search for self worth.

1:30

DIANE

I used to sneak over to the wrong side of the tracks to visit the gang from the neighbourhood we lived in before my grandad died. I had a ton of friends down there. Summertime the rich kids and the poor kids could mix it up. Was the schools kept us apart. We'd sit on a stoop and sing the songs from the hit parade and eat popsicles and neck. Sometimes someone's parents would be out for the evening and we'd go over there and dance and we'd rub up against each other until we thought it would drive everyone nuts. On steamy summer nights we'd all go strut out on St. Catherine Street. One time we went up to Beaver Lake. They had dancing out there. A man asked me to dance. He was European, or maybe ... I don't know, but he had a heavy accent and he was much older than the boys in our group. He was dark and very handsome and very grown-up. I didn't know the dances, and very patiently he showed me how. When we stopped, finally, all my friends were gone. He walked me all the way home, asking a million questions about me. He was very interested ... he wanted to know everything about me ... or so it seemed ... then he kissed me, very lightly on the lips and disappeared. I never knew his name, or saw him again, but for years he was the focus of all my erotic fantasies. I'd dream that he was waiting for me at the lake, in a uniform and I'd be in some gauzy pale gown and we would dance for hours under the stars and then he would make mad passionate love to me and show me how everything went, like when he was so patient teaching me to dance. Then we would lie there naked and panting under the trees.

Available from Playwrights Union of Canada as a copyscript.

A PARTICULAR CLASS OF WOMEN

by Janet Feindel

*A funny, poignant, bawdy series of dynamic characters in-
spired by women in striptease, in monologue format.*

1:30

LIL

Well, I mustta had something. For twenty-two years, I manage to
turn guys on. I mustta had something. Whatever it was that turned
them on, I had it. I can still turn on an eighteen-year-old no
problem. I was the best stripper in Canada. I could have been a
professional, like a doctor or a lawyer. But people are too stupid to
realize that. They think just because you come from Timmins, you
got no culture. Well, we had culture, believe you me. I worked in
the theatre there. We built a theatre out of a barn and every summer
we put on the plays; *MOUSETRAP, CHARLIE'S AUNT, ARSENIC
AND OLD LACE* ... so art's not new to me. You know what? The
straight theatre don't pay. I work in the theatre now but I don't work
as an actress. What do I want to be an actress for? I been on the
stage for twenty two years. Being a stripper was just another part. I
was an entertainer! There's a history to this business. Even the girls
today, they don't realize we're part of show business, part of a
tradition. Like this one girl I work with; beautiful black chick,
lovely long legs, good show, nice girl but she don't even know who
Dionne Warwick is! She barely even heard of the Warwick Hotel
and that was a Toronto landmark. We used to call it the Airwick or
the Whorewick. We had more fun there. I work all across Canada as
a stripper and it was the best place. Except for the places in
Montreal! I love to work Montreal. People put those places down
because they are run by the mafia. Well, *I like* to work for mafia. I
work in Montreal for years. Do the clubs get busted the way they do
here? NO! Who protects you? The mafia! And when my daughter
Rosie was sick, before medicare, who paid the hospital bill?

Maurice, club owner, mafia! *And* I had one friend, wanted to give up stripping, become a bartender, who give her job retraining? The mafia! How long do you suppose it would have taken the government to do that for her? I tell you, I would rather work for the mafia any day. They know how to look after their people. Where would Frank Sinatra be, if it wasn't for the mafia?

Published by Lazara Publishing—trade paperback.
Distributed in Canada by Blizzard Publishing and Playwrights Union of
Canada. Distributed in the U.S. by Inland Book Co., P.O. Box 120261,
East Haven, Conn., 06512.

MARK

by Betty Jane Wylie

A doctor and his family must learn to face the fact of his terminal illness. The play tackles the subject of death with uncompromising honesty.

1:20

KATE

Suddenly when something's wrong, when you've really got trouble, people treat you as if you've got leprosy. Not that they won't associate with you, but you might as well be the person you were yesterday, or not there at all, for all they'll talk to you about the only thing you can think about. Because all you can think, as you go about the ordinary business of living is, my father is dying, my father is dying, my father is dying, and I love him. O Lord—and then you stop, because you must never ask why. I don't know how I know that but I do. You must never ask why. You know why. He has cancer, that's why. So you must only say thank you. My father is dying and thank you that he lived. But people don't want to talk to you about that. They want to talk to you about other things. And they don't want you to talk about it either. So they hedge you about with words and things and offer you a drink or coffee or a cigarette or friendship and you don't want to hear it. In this luxurious antibiotic century, to be threatened is to be shamed. How dare you suffer? We all go around pretending nothing is going to happen to us and you come along with that long face letting us know it's all a pretence. You're destroying our smugness, you're threatening our safety, so don't. Don't talk about it.

Published by Playwrights Canada Press as a bound playscript.

THE FIGHTING DAYS

by Wendy Lill

*Set in the 1910's, the play follows Frances Beynon's journey
into the Winnipeg feminist movement, where she eventually
clashes with Nellie McClung over pacifism and universal
suffrage.*

1:30

NELLIE

My name is Nellie McClung and I'm a disturber. Disturbers are
never popular. Nobody likes an alarm clock in action, no matter
how grateful they are later for its services! But I've decided that I'm
going to keep on being a disturber. I'm not going to pull through life
like a thread that has no knot. I want to leave something behind
when I go; some small legacy of truth, some word that will shine in
a dark place. And I want that word to be ... DEMOCRACY!
Democracy for Women. Because I'm a firm believer in Women, in
their ability to see things and feel things and improve things. I
believe that it is Women who set the standards for the world and it is
up to us, the Women of Canada, to set the standards ... HIGH!
Maybe I'm sort of a dreamer, maybe I'm sort of naive ... but I look
at my little girls and boys and I think I want a different world for
them than the one I was born into. I look at them and my heart cries
out when I see them slowly turn towards the roles the world has
carved for them: my girls, a life of cooking and sewing and
servicing the needs of men; and the boys, scrapping and competing
in the playground, then right up into the corridors of government, or
even worse, the battlefields. I want them to have a choice about
their lives. We mothers are going to fight for the rights of our little
girls to think and dream and speak out. We're going to refuse to
bear and rear sons to be shot at on faraway battlefields. Women
need the vote to bring about a better, more equitable, peaceful
society, and we're going to get it!

Published by Talon Books—trade paperback.

have no anecdotes, humourous or insightful, about auditions. They're horrendous for everyone involved but unfortunately are the best thing we've been able to devise to date.

I'm sure your new book of Canadian audition monologues will be useful for many of our young actors. Please do refer, somewhere, to the fact that these are for reference and information only and do not take the place of a thorough study of the play as a whole.

Martha Henry
Artistic Director
The Grand Theatre
London, Ontario

IDYLL GOSSIP

by Carol Sinclair

The play celebrates the courage of rural Nova Scotian women who dare to dream of forming a musical group. Warning: contains subject matter dealing with battered women, loneliness and laundry.

1:00

WANDA

Well jees. Meet me at the morgue. I mean, as if my life was going the way I planned it. I've had two husbands. Count 'em. Two. Neither of which ever bothers to send a letter, never mind a cheque! I've got a hyperactive baby my own mother says is homely enough to sour milk. I've got Raylene living in, she doesn't have enough smarts to blow her own nose hardly, but I suspect she's doing a brisk bit of business behind the school. I've got a house the termites can't be bothered with, a dog with the mange and a car I call The Exorcist. Barn takes me bowling twice a month, so long as I pay.

Real bowl of cherries I picked out for myself ... So who am I to give advice ...

Well ... I got the store. That's it. I got a store ... Wanda's Variety and Fresh Meats is the joy of my life. Can't exactly curl up at night with the account books, know what I mean?

You could put all the romance and excitement I've had in my life inside a paper cup and step on it ... Buncha bums ...

Available from Playwrights Union of Canada as a copyscript.

SMOKE DAMAGE

by Baṇuta Rubess

A vacation in Europe becomes a quest as five women visit the landmarks where nine million women perished as witches between the 15th and 17th centuries. Wicked humour is blended with fact, fairy tale and quotes from the Church's handbook for witch hunters.

2:00

ANNA KÄSER

My name is Anna Käser. Käser, K-A, Anna, Anna Käser. I am forty years old. I have five children. I have five children, three of them died, three of my children died. Oh Jesus Christ be with me, Dear God open your heart to me. I am thirsty. No, I am not a witch. I am no witch. (*laughing*) These accusations are all lies. I am innocent. No, I do not wish to die. Whatever is God's wish is my wish and as I am innocent I gladly accept death. Whatever is God's wish is my wish and as I am innocent I gladly accept death.

(*glancing over her shoulder*) No, it's not a devil's mask. I swear to you I've had it since I was a child. I swear … I'm thirsty.

(*shouting*) I'm a witch. Yes, yes I am guilty. Dear God open your heart. The devil gave me ointments. Black and green powder. I smeared the ointment on a cherry and gave it to my son and he died. Yes, yes, I put it into a stew and gave it to my baby and he caught the plague and died.

(*pausing*) A knife, please. My collar is so tight. A knife, please. I am innocent. What I told you about my children was all lies.

Yes, yes, the devil comes to me at night. He came to me as a hangman. Intercourse is so painful. I think my back and thighs are falling apart. Yes, he comes to me here in prison. He tries to pull my tongue out. To make me strangle myself with my finger down my throat. See my eyes are black and blue where he has poked them.

I'm so thirsty. Oh Jesus Christ be with me dear God open your heart to me I am innocent.

- 84 -

The devil ordered me to commit suicide. Yes, my right arm, I tried to scratch the vein open. Yes, I flew to the sabbat. Yes, yes, I had many accomplices. Yes, I raised many tempests, five, no, eight, no—

Nothing I've said is true.

————

Published by Playwrights Canada Press—trade paperback.

IF BETTY SHOULD RISE

by David Demchuk

*Four sisters give drastically different accounts of the diffi-
cult childhood they shared, revealing a past fraught with
physical, emotional and sexual abuse.*

1:45

ADDIE

Daddy died the first week of July in 1960, early in the morning, in
the garage. Heart attack. In another week he would've been
sixty-four. Momma … Momma called me around ten thirty that
morning, very calm, like it was something that had happened years
ago, or had happened to someone else, a neighbour, a stranger … I
called Ted and Bill—Ted in Victoria with his wife, Bill in
Emerson—and Rose and Vera and Betty. Betty took it the hardest,
she always fancied herself Daddy's pet, I had to go over to her place
for the afternoon to, you know, to be with her … I was afraid she
might do something. She and I took the train up to Momma's
together, though in the end she was too upset to go to the ceremony,
stayed in the house, in our old room, crying.

Rose drove in from that reserve she lives on with that fool husband
of hers. And Vera, well, she said she had trouble arranging the time
off and would drive up on the day. Two hours we held the service
up waiting for her and she never showed, Momma was beside
herself, thought there'd been an accident. No phone call, no
nothing. I called her place on a hunch and there she was, drunk. No
surprises in our family. I tore strips off of her, I can tell you, and she
bawled and nattered away … and that's when she started with the
lies. Daddy did this, Daddy did that, garbage like I've never heard
before in my life, drunken garbage and I told her exactly that.

I hung up, heard a noise behind me. Rose was standing in the
doorway, for how long … I pushed past her and went out into the
yard, then down back behind the shed where I'd gone years before
with my handful of clover and snapdragons … I looked towards the

wood, my neck prickled as the stories, about the dogs in the woods came back, though the dogs themselves must've been long gone. I stopped and stood behind the shed, looking down at the place where I'd once knelt ... I heard Rose come up behind me—she stayed well back, but still I heard her, and I turned around. I must've been crying. She said to me, she said ...

She said ... Nothing ... just ... she just ... held me ... told me I was right, told me that Vera was lying, always had ... always ... and that's all. Nothing.

Available from Playwrights Union of Canada as a copyscript.

PEGGY'S SONG

by Jim Garrard

An attractive, middle-aged woman suffering the loss of her son, discovers that her husband, recently killed in a plane crash, had been seeing another woman. She hires a seedy detective to exorcise her demons.

2:25

PEGGY

We met in high school, Howard and I. I was the brain and he was the bad apple. I think my parents worried more that I might marry him than they did about me catching cold. He was a great one for the girls. Once, when a bunch of us were working on some project or other—I think we were painting banners for student elections—Howard showed up late with his girlfriend of that time. She was a cheerleader. They came in the door and went straight across the room—we were in some kind of ethnic hall—and into a smaller room that had an old armchair in it, the big, stuffed kind. He was wearing a leather windbreaker and cowboy boots. They fell into the chair in each other's arms and for a moment I could see them framed, from where I stood, by the doorway. His foot came up and touched the open door and pushed it shut. I must have stared at that closed door for a least five minutes. Talk about dumbfounded!

That was nearly twenty-five years ago, but it's still as clear as a bell in my mind's eye. It's wonderful the feelings we have as kids when we're in love for the first time. I was crazy about Howard for a whole year after I watched him kick that door shut. And he had no idea. We had the same home room the next year. Whenever he spoke to me, which got to be quite often, my neck and chest would flush bright red. Like beets. It wasn't just the colour rising up my body that was embarrassing: I'd also get very hot and have difficulty breathing, and I'd say the *stupidest* things. My god! People who don't blush don't know what it is to be mortified.

That year, Howard was running for student president and I was a lowly volunteer in his organization. One Saturday night, on my birthday, actually, there I was in Deer Park clubhouse making posters and painting banners. Howard was holding court. I was absolutely sure I didn't exist for him as far as a romance was concerned. But miracles do happen.

This night, there were about twenty other students in the room, including Howard. There was a light switch by the door that controlled all the lights. For some reason I will never understand. I went over to that switch and turned it off. Next thing I knew I was in the centre of that room, in the pitch dark, in Howard's arms. We must have felt the exact same thing at the exact same moment in order to find each other in the dark like that. It was magic. I don't know what the others must have thought. I don't remember the lights coming back on. I just remember his arms around me. I remember kissing him. I remember his chest against my breasts. I remember him driving me home in his car and coming up to the door with me and kissing me goodnight. If that wasn't heaven, it couldn't be better.

Available from Playwrights Union of Canada as a copyscript.

MY RUMANIAN COUSIN

by Aviva Ravel

Seniors Max and Ethel have their staid notions thrown into a state of flux when their eccentric, much-married cousin Clara comes to visit.

1:50

CLARA

I have such an exciting day! First I go on the bus all over the city. To St. Denis and Ste. Catherine, Ville LaSalle and Verdun, and Ste. Helen Island. The bus drivers are very helpful and charming. There is a sign says not to talk to them, but we ignore that. Then I go to a big department store and buy beautiful material for your dresses—purple and yellow, orange and red. Then I visit the Mechanical Marvels downtown. Such a splendid store! I meet all the customers and clerks, but not the Manager, Sam, he is too busy because there is a big sale with a 12%. But I meet an extraordinary gentleman, and he invites me for lunch. I already eat lunch with all the bus drivers, but I have a second small lunch with him.

Of course I cannot be serious for him because he is seventy-five years old. But we have a good conversation. His name is ... like flowers in French ... Lafleur? No ... Laviolette? No ... Larose? No ... Latulippe? No, it is lots of flowers. Ah, Desjardins!

Such a nice gentleman. But I say I cannot meet him again, there is no future for me with a man seventy-five years old since I am only forty-five. Then I see a language school! So I go right in and enlist. I even buy books and a notebook. See? Such a nice teacher. The name is ... like a fruit with a little insect. An orange? A pear? No ... A plum? No ... An apple? Yes, that's it! Apple-by. (*pronounced Apple-bee*)

So he invites me for dinner. Such a nice gentleman. We have a good conversation but I say I cannot meet him again in private because there is no future for me with a man twenty-five years old. When I am sixty, he is only forty, and that is asking for trouble. But he is very handsome. He drives me home in a Jaguar that belongs to his father.

Yes, Montreal is beautiful. Beautiful scenery and beautiful people. Well, I go to my room to unpack the parcels. I will show you the material in a jiffy.

———————

Available from Playwrights Union of Canada as a copyscript.

CLAUDIUS

by Ken Gass

*Gertrude, awakening to the possibility that her first hus-
band may have been murdered, stares into an urn contain-
ing his ashes.*

2:35

GERTRUDE

Why did he burn my husband's body? Odd words. Husband.
Burn...(*peering into the urn*) Darling Theodore. Is this really you? All
that's left? I remember...What? Almost nothing, as if ... (*beat*) You
were my first lover, my only lover until—Why did I—No, don't go
back, mustn't...(*beat*) Oh, Theo, poor baby Theo...You died, didn't
you? Ended your life, gave me freedom to—Why? Because you knew I
was unfaithful? With your brother? Shouldn't I be suffering guilt now?
Claudius doesn't. I don't think. But why did he burn my husband's
body? Are you my husband? Still? Did you end your life, or...? No, I
dare not, must not, musn't believe...(*pause*)

I want to remember you, Theodore. I want to, but - It's as if you never
existed. Strange, how I feel absolutely no guilt about that either. Of
course, if there was a god, I could feel guilt. Guilt would have purpose
then, meaning. But there's only ashes. That's all, obviously, that we
are...

But I do take responsibility. And remember...marrying you, and the
purity I felt the first time you touched me, and yes, how gentle you
were, yes, and your breath smelled of lilac that night...No, Claudius
wears lilac, you wore...I can't remember, remember only
the sweetness of it...and your body, thin, frail almost, but firmly
muscled, and, yes, I remember your beard, softer than Claudi's, and
very blue eyes, no, grey, grey like the stones I gave you, and yes,
you made me pregnant, and I remember the pain of giving birth to
Hamlet, and the waters breaking, and, you laughing, but why is
everything else like a foggy sea, like a pale, empty parchment...

Why did he burn my husband's body? What am I supposed to do with these ashes? A mantle-piece ornament? Poor Theodore, locked in a jar like a Persian genie. How do I let you out?

(*sitting on the floor and reaching into the jar, touching the ash and putting it to her lips*) Yes. I can taste you. Even your smell is coming back to me. The smell of your beautiful soft skin, against mine, and our bodies' fluids, that strange odour, the first time we —

(*pressing the urn against her breast, as Claudius enters*) Why did you burn my husband's body?

———

Available from Playwrights Union of Canada as a copyscript.

I'm really sorry I'm late but I was stuck in the streetcar.

THE MELVILLE BOYS

by Norm Foster

Owen and Lee Melville arrive at their uncle's lakeside cabin for a weekend of beer and fishing, but their plans are thrown out of whack by the arrival of two sisters. The women stay the night and become catalysts for a funny and unsentimental look at four lives in transition.

1:40

MARY

Well, let me tell you something, mister. Don't start preaching to me about how things can't be the way they used to be, because I, for one, am counting on it. And if I want to sit around for two years, or five years, or ten years and wait for some clown to come home with my car, then I'll goddamn wait! And if, for some reason, I get it in my mind that I want to go out on a date, then I'll go out. And don't you tell me this isn't a date. Don't you dare. Your brother stood right here and asked us if we'd go with you, and we said yes.

I don't care whose idea it was. We went! We had dinner with you. We danced with you. We put dresses on. How many women did you see there tonight with dresses on? Three! Me, Loretta, and Mrs. Gunther, who's a cow and can't fit into a pair of pants anyway. So, don't tell me this isn't a date. I haven't been out with a man in two years, and I don't appreciate the fact that the first time I do go out, it gets passed off as a car pool. It's a date! And it's not over yet. So, you'd better start showing me a good time, and pretty goddamn fast!

(*pausing*)I guess I lost my temper there. I don't do that very often. I can usually keep it under control. As a matter of fact, that used to drive my husband crazy. He'd get mad at something, and I'd stay calm. And the calmer I stayed … the madder he got. Maybe I should've got mad more often.

Published by Playwrights Canada Press—trade paperback.

PEGGY'S SONG

by Jim Garrard

An attractive, middle-aged woman suffering the loss of her son, discovers that her husband, recently killed in a plane crash, had been seeing another woman. She hires a seedy detective to exorcise her demons.

2:10

PEGGY

I was attending a committee meeting of the A.G.O. when I got the news. Two women came to the boardroom to tell me I had a phone call in the executive director's office. The carpet is very soft up there and they weren't making any noise as they came toward me. It's just as they say: I knew before I was out of my chair that Howard was dead. How do you explain that sort of thing? He was in perfect health. I wasn't even worried he'd be flying around in that goddamned airplane of his. I figured he was safe on the ground in New York City. But he wasn't. He was lying dead beside a lake three hundred miles north of Toronto. When I think of all the ridiculous things we did together in our lifetime—all the things that added up to two people knowing each other so well that one of them could draw an unthinkable conclusion from the sight of two strangers crossing a room—I have to think that can only have something to do with what love is. But when I think about the woman who died with him—whoever she was—or, maybe, I should say girl—she was only a teenager—and when I think how sordid the story seemed in the papers, there are times when I can't help myself.

You bastard, I say. Out loud. Quite often. I can't help wondering who she was and what she had to do with Howard. I didn't at first. But things lodge in the brain and grow there. I've had six months to think about this and now I know I'll never have another thought if I don't get rid of this one. I guess the loveliest part was getting to look at them both. An O.P.P. cruiser came to my door and drove me downtown somewhere. Near Yonge Street. We drove into a basement where there was a coldroom full of drawers. The contents of Howard's drawer were well-known to me, but I'd never laid eyes on that poor girl before. If you think cops are unimaginative, it's not true. These guys managed to ask me the same questions in about one hundred and fifty different ways and never invented the slightest notion about who she was. They wouldn't admit it to me, but I know they closed their books on the whole affair when the detective who was handling the case went on holiday. By the middle of January they'd stopped returning my calls. It was clear to me they had no interest in this mystery. But I was interested. So I hired a private investigator. He turned out to be the most disgusting man in the world. But he helped me.

Available from Playwrights Union of Canada as a copyscript.

LOKKINEN

by Barbara Sapergia

*A man's obsession with his Finnish ancestry and his fanta-
sies about a northern farm almost destroy the four women
who share a house with him.*

1:45

MRS. McBRIDE

I loved being a bride. Isabel was my maid of honour, and she was so
jealous, I could tell … We didn't wear white then. I had a dress of
ivory satin, it was the prettiest dress I'd ever seen, with brown silk
piping … I had a good figure, Douglas could almost clasp his hands
around my waist …

He looked so fine in his suit and waistcoat. His hair was all slicked
down, I remember it was still a little bit damp, and he smelled clean,
like soap. They asked him, "Do you, Douglas Andrew McBride take
this woman?" "I do," he said, and they could hear him in the back
of the church. Everyone remarked on it, how Doug had spoken out
so clear. Of course, that was Doug all over …

I remember that first little house, with the lilacs by the front gate …
and Doug was working as a clerk at the Garrett's Men's Store, and
he'd walk home for lunch every day. Doug said we'd get a better
house some day, when we started a family. Only we waited and
waited, but no babies came. Doug never said anything, but I knew
he was disappointed, and so was I. I'd given up hope when I found
out I was carrying Perlie. I was thirty-five years old, and I 'd given
up all hope …

They tell you all babies look the same, all red and wrinkled and
crying, but Perlie wasn't like that at all … his face was smooth and
he had curling black hair, right from the start, and he could laugh
and smile, right from the start … But sometimes he got sick and
cranky, and then he'd keep me up in the night … I was so tired then,
I just didn't seem to have my old strength … and Perlie'd be crying
his lungs out, and Doug, in the clear voice of his, he says in my ear,

"Can't you see what ails the child?" And I'd pick the baby up, but I couldn't stop the crying …

But he was a good man, Doug was. In forty years of marriage, he never once spoke in anger … he believed in self-control. And he always gave me enough to run the house … Only after he was gone, I got so confused. Once we'd covered him in earth, I couldn't seem to remember his face … except I could still see him as he was the day we married.

Published by Playwrights Canada Press—trade paperback.

LILLY, ALTA.

by Kenneth Dyba

Two lovers attempting to free themselves from the ruling matriarch of Lilly, Alta. unleash a chain of events forever altering the small town which is peopled by many colourful characters, such as Honey Gullacher and her cat Chaucer.

1:50

HONEY GULLACHER

I'd just finished pourin' Austin a cup of tea. Dugald was sittin' with me in the kitchen, havin' his lunch before he raced back to school … Austin was fixin' some loose shingles on the roof right there, right over your head, Chaucer. He didn't have to do it that day, it was so miserable out. Snow blowin' like hellfire. But Austin knew them shingles was botherin' me so he was fixin' 'em. Dugald's just pointin' some of his spellin' out to me when we hear a regular rushin' of wind and Austin's voice callin' to me from every part of the world it seems like. Dugald and me, we run outside. There's Austin, stretched out in the snow, his head smashed open on a rock. The ladder's tipped over on its side and the snow—it's turnin' red. Mrs. Lilly's on her horse, snow blowin' round her like it was some kind of fancy perfume. Mrs. Lilly, she trots off. (*pausing*)

Why'd I ever force Austin to come to Lilly? He wanted to set down in the Okanagan. We could have sprouted roots there just as easy. Been happy. Why Lilly? Why'd I ever choose Lilly? *Lilly?* Name sounded so pretty. Then.

We come from Portsmouth on November 3rd, 1928, and on December 17th, 1932, Austin leaves me. We were a real family—Austin, and Dugald, and me. Wasn't our fault Quenten Boone couldn't beget his own kin with her … Why'd she have to come bargainin' with my Austin for our next one? Only we never had a next one … After Dugald died in the service of his country in '43 and they send me that telegram sayin' there wasn't enough of him left to ship home for me to bury, I told Austin that I was gonna live to make it right with him and Dugald for ever forcin' 'em to come to Lilly.

———

Published by Playwrights Canada Press—trade paperback.

THE MAIL ORDER BRIDE

by Robert Clinton

An absurdist comedy which simultaneously explores three generations of the Teeter family and the farm that figures in their lives.

2:00

EVA

I was at the High Commission in London during the Battle of Britain, secretary to Russell's mother. She was ... so ... important. To think that I was working with her, I was just in ... (*pausing*) I was very lucky. Caught up in something so big. I met Russell at a Commission affair. The Blitz was roaring. When we came back upstairs, the staff opened the curtains in the dark ballroom, and we watched the city by the light of its own flames. Russell arrived late from night Ops. He had downed two Fighters. He smelled of cordite and petrol and ... burned brighter than the fires in the next street. I felt as silly as a moth. (*pausing*) All around me, people, friends were dying. It was ... easy to give yourself in those days. The War ended, we got married, and ... Palestine. Dutch Indonesia. Korea. Wherever the Air Force sent him. I haven't been home since. It's just that ... things used to be, during the War, things used to be ... everything was for the last time, and that made it the first time each time. There weren't many options. Now Russell is ... still the same. Or he's changed and I'm the one who has to ... (*pausing*) Husbands take a lot of getting used to. (*pausing*) What do you know about husbands? (*pausing*) Paul isn't Russell's baby. He knows. When Paul ... Russell was posted to an American aircraft carrier for four months. I know that doesn't seem long, but ... that's the way we live. And ... I went to a party at the officer's mess. One of his old flight buddies was there. I wasn't drunk. (*pausing*) I wish time could go backward. Russell? Hah. He just about ... ! In the Air Force, and the jobs he's looking for, you have to have a wife and family. Well, he's got one. Picture perfect. It ... he leaves me alone.

(*pausing*) Paul was born when Russell was in Japan on business—he'd quit the Air Force by then. He came back. I showed him Paul. He looked at him in his crib. Paul started crying. Just hungry. And Russell ... he was like a little boy. He's fought so many battles. I'd never seen him like that.

\

———

Published by Blizzard Publishing Ltd.—trade paperback.

THERESE'S CREED

by Michael Cook

A middle-aged Newfoundland widow reminisces about her past as she observes the changing world of her children.

3:00

THERESE

I minds dat time ... the year afore Pat died, when dey had mass out dere. All the families going off in the boats, sun beating the water till it shone like dat old copper pan me mother 'ad till the feller come from Toronto and give her a couple o' dollars fer it. I minds it well ... All the boats stretched out across the ocean fer seven miles, and den anchoring in the cove, and all of us saying hello, and smiling like we were met fer the first time. An' the church wor full, and we all spilled out on the grass, and the gulls and the murrs and the tansies and the puffins setting up the great din and all around the ocean ... nothing but ocean ... shining in the sun. Dey says the church be two hundred year old ... I don't know about dat ... But the winders are some old fashioned. Dey was right low, ye could see right t'rough the aisle, and from the inside all ye could see about ye was ocean still ... And dere we all was, and the priest 'ad brought loudspeakers wired to some kind o' battery, an' we said mass out dere, on Duck Island, in the sun, kneeling on the grass. Pat knelt next to me, and Walter and Marvin and Mary Francis ... She wor home den, and Morgan and Bernice ...

I believe in God the Father Almighty, Creator o' Heaven and Earth and in Jesus Christ, His only begotten Son. I minds the Creed. An' I looked across at Pat and he wor crying. I nivir durst say anyt'ing to'n. Nivir mentioned it.

(*pausing*) And after the mass, we all had a picnic, an' the fires was going an' the beer flowing ... Well, don't say we nivir had the good time. It seemed den it wor the beginning o' something, but I t'inks now, it wor the other way about. It wor the end of it, somehow. We nivir done it agin. And when I gits to the island dese days, once or twice a summer, it makes me sad to t'ink on it. Seemed like we was at the top o' some kind of curve and from den on, it wor all down hill. Pat, he knew. An' I suppose it's only jest coming to me. And I'm not sure whether I wants to know about it or not. I should jest git on, I suppose, fer a few more years and not mind nothing, till dey've gone. Till dey've all left me. I minds how Pat, the week afore he died, it wor ... I minds how he said ... It'd come on to snow something fierce ...

It'd be nice, maid, he said, if when dey's all gone, when all the youngsters on the whole bloody island has upped and gone, if dey was a nice old people's home fer us to crawl into until we dies. Think on it, he said, someone fer to wait on ye a bit, get yer meals, wake ye in the morning and tell ye when to git to bed o' nights. Don't ye t'ink dat'd be nice, maid?

An' I said I don't know, Pat, boy, I doesn't know at all. (*beginning to cry*) And dey goes and does it now, dere be no point in me going on me own boy, would dere? Well, damn dat. 'Tis raining agin. An' I suppose it rains forever dis wash is goin' out. Come on, Therese, girl. Come on. Dey's no point in grieving ... None at all. T'was long enough ago ye made yer bed, and I 'llows, ye've some time left to lie on it ...

––––––––

Published by Gage Publishing Co. Ltd.—trade paperback.

TO GRANDMOTHER'S HOUSE WE GO

by Joanna McClelland Glass

Three generations of family gather at Grandie's house in Connecticut. The tradition of the young taking care of the old is reversed as the marital anarchy of the youngest generation lays its angst and requests at the old woman's feet. Harriet is of the middle generation, a mother of three. Jared is her uncle.

2:00

HARRIET

I want you to listen to what I have to say, and please, please accept it as the last word on this matter. Many years ago, when you were toddlers, I had an encounter with an older woman in the park. She watched us for a while, on the swings, and then she came over and chatted. Her face wasn't noticeably wrinkled but her eyes told a different story. I thought I'd never seen anyone with so much mileage in the eyes. As she left, she said, "You can only be as happy as your unhappiest child." Time proved her right. All through puberty — all through college — all through your marriages, her words were etched on my mind. They've been like a noose around my neck. Well, now I'm the older woman. I've been quite astonished lately, at the mileage in my eyes. I have to make some changes and I can't hang on through the summer. You may stay here until Christmas. Jared and I will move in January, and then you must fend for yourselves. If you want to see me you can invite me to your homes, or come to Barlowe and take me out to dinner. I will not slave over a hot stove for your visits. I will not knit mittens for grandchildren. (*beat*) You don't want to hear this, do you? It sounds harsh and unloving, as if I'm cutting the umbilical cord. Withdrawing the nipple. Depriving. I'm sorry. But I'm fifty-seven years old and I won't ask your permission to take my life back. I love you very much. A change of location won't change my feelings. It remains to be seen what it does it does to yours. I'll see you at supper.

———

Available from Samuel French Inc. as a playscript—see Publishers' Page.

MONKEYSHINES

by Suzanne Finlay

Stuart has secretly been in love with Dorothy for twenty-five years. As she is now apparently a widow, he returns to her doorstep with hopes of finally winning her heart. Their new-found romance rejuvenates the bloom of their faded youth.

1:10

DOROTHY

I don't bother getting my hair done since Harold ... I mean, nobody out here fixes up in summer. And from Labour Day to the end of school, I don't see anybody but raccoons and squirrels. They don't care what I look like as long as I feed them.

I got so I hated New York. But when your husband's a heart surgeon, it pays to live in a high-stress area.

I didn't like it for the same reason I don't go to the beauty parlor. All the glitter and pizazz and ... phoney expectations. You make an appointment for Friday, and all through the week you're telling yourself, "Come Friday, I'll go down to Elizabeth Arden's. I'll go in looking like plain old me. But when I come out! Wars will be waged and men will die with my name on their lips!" And for an hour or two on Friday, they make you believe it. They iron out your wrinkles with cucumber squeezings, and put a shine on your hair with perfumed horse placenta. You sail home, feeling like Helen of Troy. And your son says, "Dinner's late, Mom!" And your daughter says, "I'm borrowing that dress you can't get into." And your husband slips you 50 bucks and says, "Dorothy, give yourself a treat and go to the beauty parlor." Ha! Listen to me gabble on. Mother always said I was better than a phonograph record.

Published in "Four New Comedies" by Playwrights Canada Press—trade paperback.

1949

by David French

Newfoundland is about to join Confederation. The Mercer family is reunited for the occasion—and sparks fly as they examine their lives and mourn the passing of their way of life.

2:40

RACHEL

I went over all the letters he'd sent me that time he was wounded at the Somme. They'd shipped him back to England, remember, to the hospital there ... In the first of those letters he mentioned how kind the nurses was, one in particular, and how she was even writing the letter for him. That's when I saw again the name that would prey on my mind the rest of my married life: Betty Driscoll ... Yes, it was all there in those letters, as plain as the nose on my face, only I'd never picked up on it before.

There was even a part of me could understand. I wasn't fool enough to expect he'd never look at another woman, being away like that all those years. I just never expected him to carry her picture home and wear it so brazenly around his neck. That's what angered me the most. That's the part I couldn't forgive ... And as the years went by, I'd imagine what she looked like, this Nursing Sister, this Betty Driscoll. Sometimes she'd be small and slight and soft-spoken; other times she'd be coarse. But no odds how she looked, she'd always be dressed in that starched white skirt with its sky blue blouse and black shoes ... And with time I hardened my heart to him, little by little, out of the hurt I was feeling ... One summer's night the smell of honeysuckle woke me, and I saw him at the open window, but there was too much pride in me, and the distance was too great ... And then the cancer struck him, and he bore that, too, in the only way he could, in silence. And just before the end, he turned his face towards me, working his eyes as though he was trying to tell me somet'in. Only now he didn't have the strength to speak, not even if he wanted to ...

On the last night of his wake I went up to the bedroom and took down those letters from the top shelf of the closet. I read each one again that Betty Driscoll had scribbled in her neat little hand from that hospital room in England. And then I burnt them. I marched downstairs and flung them in the stove. Then I went to the casket and gazed down at Esau. I raised the flat of my hand to strike him ... I didn't, though. Instead I took the locket off his neck and opened it, and in the light of the lamp I studied the face of the young woman inside. It wasn't even a pretty face in particular. And the camera had caught her squinting into the sun, which made her look far too serious. A little grim, even ... but I could recall the day he'd snapped that picture, Esau, and how the wind had lifted the hem of my skirt in the road outside the house ...

Oh, yes, it was my picture all those years. And suddenly I realized: those letters ... his silences ... even the look in his eyes at the end ... all of it misunderstood. The only real t'ing, as it turned out, was the shame I felt at that moment, and the remorse I've lived with ever since.

Published by Talon Books—trade paperback.

BAG BABIES

by Allan Stratton

Katie Hughes is a larger-than-life Talk Show Host and media celebrity extraordinaire. She delivers this soliloquy— a "moment of self-reflection"—to the audience, smack front and centre. On spike heels, she's Tammy Faye Baker with the personality of Bette Midler–Tallulah Bankhead, glamourous, gutsy, and direct. Earnest and committed. A Saleable package. A star!

1:50

KATIE

Don't tell me, I know. One look at me and you think, "YES! now that's GLAMOUR!" Gimmee a break! This isn't glamour. This is horseshit held together with Scotch tape and a prayer. Take the eyelashes. We're talkin' two feet long. Natural? They're not even human! Know what they are? THEY'RE MOOSE! So you say to me, "Katie, what happened? You were at Woodstock, lived in a commune, practically had *The Desiderata* tattooed on your forehead — so what's the deal? Did you sell out for money-fame-slash-success?" No. The deal is: I had a revelation. (*confidentially*) It happened when I became a star. See, before then I didn't wear wigs. I had my *own* hair. And when I say "hair" I mean "HAIR". BIG hair. Hair you could wave at pep rallies. But the day I hit primetime, bingo, the network frizzed, dyed, teased, permed and basically nuked the shit out of it. Next morning, I wake up, my hair's all over the apartment. I mean, I wake up and I am, like, bald. Yul Brynner bald. It's on the pillow, in the bathtub, I'm having breakfast it's falling in my cereal. So there I am, this bald TV star sobbing in the bathroom and I stare in the mirror and I say, "Katie, wake up! Children are starving and what do you do? You stuff yourself sick at power lunches then run to the toilet to throw up so you won't get fat. I MEAN, KATIE, GET A LIFE!" And that's when it happened: this blinding flash of light, this heavenly choir and this EPIPHANY; It's *because* I dress for success that the fans in

TV-land watch me. And because they watch me, I can tell them about world hunger, the environment and the neutron bomb. Glamour and glitz have given me a platform! A vehicle to help change the world! I, Katie Hughes, can make a difference! My life has meaning! Substance! Integrity! Do I suffer? Yes, yes, a thousand times yes! But I do it gladly. It's my responsibility to my public. This image is a sacred trust! And being bald is a small price to pay to save the world.

Published by Coach House Press—trade paperback.

ENDANGERED SPECIES
Prim and Duck, Mama and Frank

by Margaret Hollingsworth

A mother, her two adult children and a mysterious uncle struggle with questions of self-identity, social acceptance and perceptions of reality.

1:45

MAMA

Such a band he has my Osvaldo. Music. Music is beauty. Music is poetry. Music is … sound. (*pausing*) That's what music is. Music is love. You wanna know about love, you just ask your Mama. Here (*pointing her foot for a massage*) Just do the toes a bit huh? Gentle now. Make it nice for your Mama.

Seeing is believing your Papa used to say, yes, but is believing seeing that's what I wanna know, is believing seeing? No? You can answer me that one? (*looking at her foot*) You got the foot of a Greek statue your Papa used to say—what's wrong with Rome I say? Nothin', he says, but the Greeks … they got there first. You mean it's an old foot, I say? No, he says, that there one is a helluva classy foot—that there is perfection in feet, that is a foot that never has to stand for its living … so much he knows huh?

I'm on that foot all day today and how much business you think we done huh? One lousy ashtray, $3.95. You know the one … the one with the head of San Antonio from the front window, looks like Mussolini, how come someone wanna butt out his cigarette on the nose of San Antonio huh? It's none of my business. Guy what buys it is Portuguese anyways. This goes on, Signor Zanoni … he's gonna close up the store then where we are? He closes, I'm gonna get me that ruby tableware, I don't care what … he's gonna give me that ruby tableware … every time some person comes in and starts lookin' at it I feel my hairs jump. You take the food outa my kids' mouth Zanoni I will be saying, you close up the store and make my little ones starve, then they shall be starving on ruby tableware.

Glass so you can see the world through, red like blood. Oh he'll see the tunnel at the end of the light, he's not as dumb as he paints himself to be that man ... he's pretty smart cookie you know that?

———————

Published by Act One Publishing—trade paperback.

THE DIRTY OLD WOMAN

by Dale Colleen Hamilton

Lizzy is a storyteller and farmer in the year 2150. She appears to be quite elderly, although certain movements suggest that she has retained her youthful energy.

4:00

LIZZY

The time I remember best is The Thunder Storm—The Simulated Thunder Storm. What a show! Thunder echoed from camouflaged speakers and fluorescent lightning flashed under The Dome. One bolt of lightning came dangerously close, carefully calculated, of course, to striking the largest of the trees in the Rainforest Memorial Museum. Then the rain came. Most of the people visiting The Pleasure Dome had never felt rain before. They'd been born and raised in PADs and all they knew of rain was the acid drizzle running down the other side of a window pane. (*breaking into song, lounge-lizard style*) I'm singing in the rain, just singin' in the rain. What a glorious feeling', I'm hap hap happy again. (*pulling out of her musical moment*) At The Pleasure Dome, on the day of The Simulated Thunder Storm, umbrellas and galoshes were available for hire. When they turned on the rain in the control tower above, those who had umbrellas raised them, as instructed. The rest ran to makeshift shelters, as instructed, to escape the downpour. It wasn't a cold rain, they made sure of that, so people weren't in any hurry to take shelter. The children stayed outside playing in the engineered mud puddles, provided at no extra charge. I was a teenager and I wanted to go with the adults, so I followed along to one of the shelters. It was tiny and it had a tin roof and the rain set up a rhythm that nobody'd ever heard before—random, unsynchronized, unpredictable. We didn't really DO anything there in the rain; that's what was so exciting. It was very crowded and there were no walls, so everybody had to huddle close together to stay dry. I was sandwiched between a man and a woman; strangers. The man was pressing up hard against me and that left no choice but for me to press up hard against the woman in front of me. Nobody seemed to mind being so close. And I could feel the man behind me breathing down my spine and some of his breath found its way into my ear. And the woman in front of me shivered every time the lightning struck and she rocked back and forth, touching me, then easing away, every time the thunder rolled. I could smell the smell of the man's shirt behind me, wet wool and it rubbed up against my bare shoulder until I couldn't tell anymore if it felt good, or if I was in pain. But I pressed closer. The woman's perfume couldn't mask the smell of her sweat. There were so many human smells in that shelter that you could sink your teeth into the air and take a big bite and roll it around, savour it, almost swallow it, then savour it some more. The storm was building, still hadn't found its release, and the rain rhythm on the roof was getting faster 'till it was solid sound that you could touch and just when you'd think that it couldn't possibly get any more intense, then it would. I couldn't get enough of that air. I was gasping in as much as my lungs would bear and I started to feel myself buckle; knees and neck first and then the rest about to follow when a final crack of thunder, bigger than all the rest combined, shook the roof and the earth and the air. At that precise moment, lightning lit up the shelter, full, complete, no dark corners, sparing no one. There was nowhere to hide from the intimacy. Then the man behind me relaxed, suddenly, complete. The woman in front of me shivered once, twice, three times—and then I felt her muscles relax against me. The storm had passed. We could hear the machinery overhead replacing thunderclouds with blue sky. The storm had passed. There was no need to continue seeking shelter. But nobody moved, nobody moved, nobody wanted to move.

Available from Playwrights Union of Canada as a copyscript.

ALBERTINE IN FIVE TIMES

by Michel Tremblay

The story of one woman at five stages of life. The older ones warn the younger of what is to come while the younger ones are full of passion and hope. Chalmers Award winner.

3:45

ALBERTINE AT 50

One day I discovered something really important. I did it myself, too, even if I'm no genius ... I was thinking about my kids and my family who never listened to me, never gave me the time of day, never asked my opinion and who treated me like I didn't exist. And I discovered that to make yourself heard in this life, you have to *disobey*. If you really want something, you *disobey*. Otherwise you get crushed. I always listened to others, took their advice, did what they wanted, you, Madeline, our two brothers, mother ... but at the age of fifty I disobeyed, and I'm not sorry.

It was hard at first ... I'd always depended on others. No kidding, if someone didn't tell me what to do, I asked. I begged! I spent my life begging. There I was, stuck in this houseful of people, and I couldn't budge until someone said it was okay. And all that did was feed my rage ... I was always about to explode. But I had this huge weight holding me back ... Marcel. Thérèse had disappeared long ago. I never heard from her except when they found her drunk in some alley, or she'd phone me from headquarters 'cause they'd just picked her up ... How many times I had to scrape together the twenty-five bucks, then take the Saint-Denis bus ... I tell this like it was nothing, but ... we get numbed by the pain, I guess ... So Marcel was all I had left, twenty-five years old, barely responsible, a child for life, who I was still protecting and would go on protecting until one of us dropped because I never could understand him ... He withdrew more and more, drifted away from me, yet still demanding I be there ... I watched him ... Yes, I watched him go mad ... I'm sorry, this isn't easy ...

I didn't stick to my role, I disobeyed. I know what you all thought, but you were wrong. If I hadn't done it, if I were still the prisoner of a madman, a madman who had me in the palm of his hand, who was growing more and more dangerous ... that's not a role for anyone. I broke the mould, I stopped being mother hen. I told Thérèse I'd have nothing more to do with her ... and I had Marcel put away, far from here ...

It hurt, but you want to know the truth? I've never been happier in my life, and neither have they. They're with their own kind, and so am I.

When it was over, and I'd done it, and I found myself alone, it was incredible. A feeling I'd never known. My days were mine, no one to worry about ... I bought new clothes, not expensive, but nice, and I went out to find a job. Do you realize what that means? A job. Freedom!

The only park I've ever known, the only bit of green, and it's mine. I work in the restaurant at parc Lafontaine, right in the very heart where everyone goes ... and they say I make the best bacon, lettuce, and tomato sandwich with mayo in the world! People come here especially for my BLT's. They come to me 'cause I'm the best! And what's more, I get paid! The customers and the other employees love me, and they treat me like a queen because I feed them like they used to get fed at home.

At least I'm not down on all fours cleaning up Marcel's mess or getting ulcers 'cause Thérèse has pulled another stunt! I come here singing in the morning, I sing while I work, and I go home singing at night. I watch the sun set in summer and the kids skating in winter. I earn my living, do you understand? I live as I please without family on my back, without kids, without men! Oh yes, no men. By choice. And I'm happy. I held myself back too long, I had to disobey!

Published by Talon Books—trade paperback. Reprinted with kind permission of J.C. Goodwin and Associates. Translated by John Van Burek and Bill Glassco.

Two years ago when I was out of work and seven months pregnant I figured that a voice-over career was what I needed. I went in to see the agent at the Talent Group who handles all the voice work.

Halfway through our meeting, I became quite overcome with the heat and then the nerves as I tried to hide my discomfort. I removed as much clothing as possible without attracting attention but the overwhelming feeling of fainting proved to be too much. I stood up, green around the gills, walked into a wall and passed out!

Needless to say, it was quite some time before I was sent out on any auditions.

Warmest,

Sheila McCarthy
Toronto, Ontario

Non-Equity auditions are down the hall.

PATCHES

by Robert More

A first-generation Ukrainian-Canadian and a fourth-generation Scottish-Canadian meet through their mutual interest in embroidering and quilting which evolves into a close and nurturing friendship. They give each other hope.

2:25

KATERINA

I brought something for you to see (*unwrapping the parcel*)—a dress. It was sent to me from Germany. It belonged to my sister. Once, it was very pretty. And look, here, a patch. I will explain that later. My mother and I, we made this dress for my sister's wedding. This is not her bride's dress, of course; but still, it is a special dress, for after, for the honeymoon. That wedding. The celebration lasted for three days; it was the biggest event of my childhood. I was only nine, so hopeful of life, and for me that wedding was a dream. Olesia was my princess, and Andrij, her husband, my handsome Cossack! To see them standing side by side, it was so beautiful you cannot imagine—are you listening? This was the dress she wore when they left the village to begin their new life; and the picture of them leaving together, the happiness shining in my sister's eyes, this picture is as clear to me now as it was then, forty years ago ... And now I will tell you about this patch. This patch means 'Untermenschen', people who are inferior. Jews wore them, as well as Slavs, and others. My sister and her husband were required to put this patch on their clothes when they were taken to the work camps. For most of the time they were together; but somehow, at the very end, became separated. Andrij searched frantically but there was no trace of my sister. She had vanished. Then, months later, he saw this dress. But it was worn by another woman. He asked this woman where she got the dress. She told him, in the market. And, of course, he knew. Olesia was dead. Like so many others, she had been shot, her clothing taken and sold.

Andrij bought the dress from this woman, and sent it to me with a letter of explanation. When I received it, my dreams died for a long time. I was a young woman, a wife, the mother of two healthy babies; I was in Canada, and I'd had enough. My family, all of them, were dead to me. I loved them, but they were gone, and I did not want to know about these things anymore. I just wanted a new life, to be left alone, in peace, with a new life. So, I put the dress into its wrapping, tied it tight with strings, put it into the bottom of an old trunk, and left it ... until today ... And now, I will tell you what I am going to do with this dress which I have carried with me for thirty-five years, which is enough. Are you listening? I am not going to put it back into a trunk. I'm not going to keep this dress at all. I'm going to cut it up into pieces, scraps; and I'm going to sew those pieces into our new wedding quilt; and I'm not going to rest until it's finished.

———

Published by Playwrights Canada Press—trade paperback.

SWEET AND SOUR PICKLES

by Ted Galay

Olenka, 57, defies custom when she invites the man she's been seeing since her husband's death to escort her to a family wedding. Her sister-in-law finds the courage to broach the subject and in the discussion that follows they reveal early dreams of breaking with tradition and, in the process, revive their childhood friendship. Winner, 1981 Drama Award, Canadian Authors' Association.

1:45

OLENKA

I know. He was kind-hearted. And loving. And every time he lost a job, he would tell me not to worry. And he would make me laugh ... and believe in him, that everything would be all right ... and then, it wouldn't be. And sometimes I hated him ... not because things went wrong ... but because he stole those happy times from me ... even the memory of them ... and I wanted them so much. All my life, I had to cover up for him, and nobody gave me anything for it.

And do you think I have no feelings? Do you think I don't cry at night, remembering how it was to have him beside me? Do you think I don't hurt? Do you think I'm not scared? Since he died, I wake up on his side of the bed. And one night I dreamed George came back, and I said, "Oh, George, they told me you were dead. I'm so glad to see you." And he said, "Move over, you're on my side of the bed." So I moved and he lay down and I woke up then, and I was on my own side of the bed, and my heart leaped because I knew he was behind me, and I reached over and it was empty. I started to shake then, and I got up and walked, but I couldn't stop shaking for half an hour. The next day I went to the doctor, and I got so bad, I thought I was dying, I didn't know what was happening to me. So he just sat with me, and I got mad, I said, "Why aren't you doing anything?" But he said it was just anxiety and sent me to a psychiatrist.

So I told him my husband had died and I couldn't sleep and he listened for a while and finally he asked me, "What kind of a stinker was your husband?"

He helped me ... to see what I already knew. At first, I didn't want to see it. I said there was nothing wrong with George, and he said, "There must be, because if you had a really good marriage, you wouldn't be mourning so long."

I didn't know that but he said people with good marriages get over it faster if one dies. So finally I said the first thing I could think of. "He wouldn't take out the garbage." And he laughed, but it was a start. And it only took two more times and he said I didn't need to come any more. And all it was was that I just had to face the facts. That George wasn't perfect.

Published by Playwrights Canada Press—trade paperback.

BEAUX GESTES ET BEAUTIFUL DEEDS

by Marie-Lynn Hammond

A young woman seeks to resolve her split identity by uncovering the truth about her grandmothers. One is a rich, flamboyant WASP, the other a poor, hardworking French-Canadian with a survivor's sense of humour. Corrine is the Francophone grandmother.

2:25

CORRINE

So me what want to know is, what is it really like in Heaven? What are they doing there right now, Moise, Calixte, Maman, Papa, my babies Lucien and Isabel? No one seems to know that much about it, en, except that people are very happy there because at last they are with le Bon Dieu. Mais l'enfer! Monsieur le curé là, he can talk for hours about the eternity of pain and torture; the flames so hot they would make your furnace seem like a block of ice; and the terrible screams of the damned because the devils force them to eat hot coals—ah! But one thing I don't understand—how come the nuns and priests know so little about heaven, and so much about hell? Ça a pas d'bon sens, ça! Anyway, it frightens me to hear them talk like that, because ever since I saw the angel (*crossing herself*) I know heaven and hell are as real as this—table! Bien sûr, you don't believe, no one did, they said I was dreaming, but I was never the kind to have my head in the clouds. H-mf! St. Thérèse d'Avila can well have seen her visions, what else does a nun have to do all day? But me—I was much too busy for that. Oh—I knew there were angels, I just never thought I would see one! ... but that summer night, there was mon p'tit Lucien—he was very sick, so crippled he could not walk, lying in a cot at the foot of my bed, so if he made a sound I was by his side; et tout d'un coup I find myself wide awake and sitting up in bed, for no reason, because everything is quiet. Then I see a pale light at the window, and something moving there. The light becomes a shape, like a man, a woman, or both together, and all silvery, the colour of moonlight. At its back, wings like a swan; and the face—ah! So strong, so peaceful. The angel moves over to the cot and gently, tenderly, he picks up Lucien, and oh! I will never forget as long as I live the sight of his poor little legs dangling over the angel's arm as they flew out into the darkness! Night filled the room again, I ran to the little bed, and oh I was so glad to see that Lucien was still there. But when I touched him, mon Dieu! Y'etait mort! Y'etait mort! Ah, when your mother or your husband dies, it is terrible, yes! But your own child! Ça c'est le pire, ça ... For a while, all I could think of was the moment when I touched that cold, still little body. But then, I thought about the angel and I knew—Lucien is in heaven, and in heaven he can run and play like he could never do here on earth. So there is a real heaven, and my son is there. I saw the angel. And I know.

Available from Playwrights Union of Canada as a copyscript.

A MAJORITY OF TWO

by Alun Hibbert

Jonathan and Sophie have very different ideas about life after retirement. They lock horns in a battle of wits and wills. As the harsh winds of a Quebec in turmoil blow through their tidy Montreal rose garden, they are forced to reassess their dreams.

1:40

SOPHIE

These last weeks you've been treating me no better than you feel you've been treated. Do you honestly think that none of this has been happening to me? Do you think I haven't been affected by the spiteful political atmosphere that's driven my children away because they saw no future for themselves here? This has been my home too. It is my home. Leaving it does not fill me full of joy. It hurts. Deeply. But you've cut me out and ignored me until I can't let you any more. I'm leaving Jonnie and you don't seem to care. I'm surprised you haven't helped me pack my bags.

But if I'm to stay, it's to be on your terms. No accommodation, no compromise. How could you just watch me go Jonnie? We've been so much together: the children, our garden, our home. What should I do? Become nostalgic and maudlin? Remember all the things we've shared and cried and laughed over together? All the bittersweet memories? Might that work? Should I talk of a time before complexities and absurdities? Seamed stockings? My father's doorway? Of saying goodbye so many, many times with complete faith that it was never forever? Or talk of tea and roses and contented company that we've had? That we've been? Would any of that work?

I wouldn't want it to work. Memories are nothing to build a future on. What's your future Jonathan? What do you want from it?

Well, to date, your only response has been to rant and rave, whine and bleat and take your frustrations out on me. Or Louis. A lot of fury signifying nothing. You pull yourself up full and square and pompously declare yourself to be English. You wrap yourself up in a flag of different colours and leave, proving yourself as much a thief in the night as the zealots claim you to be.

———————

Published by Playwrights Canada Press—trade paperback.

A FIELD OF FLOWERS

by Laurie Fyffe

After her release from a training school for girls, Alice, with her friend, Gillian, sets out to steal back the baby she believes to be rightfully hers. Against the poverty of The Depression, society's harsh moral code and corruption within the school system, can these two young women hold on to Alice's child?

2:40

GILLIAN

There was this farmer whose wife ran off on him. So, he advertised for a housekeeper, and my mother took us with her when she went to live with him on his farm. She did everything: cooking, cleaning, even worked in the barn and the fields. He didn't pay her, but we got food and clothes and a roof. Oh, he was real nice, at first. Told my brother Ryan and me to call him Uncle Will. Yes, sir, Uncle Will. (*a beat*) Well, one morning I hear my mother cryin' in the kitchen, and Uncle Will is yellin' at her. "Who do you think you are?" he says. "Woman, you just better make up your mind, see things my way, or put them two kids in the orphanage, and find yourself another job." Then, his voice went all soft, and sweet-like. I couldn't hear exactly what he was saying, but him talking all soft like that made me more scared than when he was yellin'. After that, my mother cried a lot. But any time I asked her what was up, she said it was nothing. And when I said—"So, how come yer always cryin' over nothing?" She says—Didn't we have food, and a good place to live, and to mind my own business. (*a beat*) She should have told me, you know, she should have told me what was goin' on. Anyway, this one morning my brother, Ryan, he woke up real early. Said he had this bad pain, and he started to cry. I ran to get my mother, but she wasn't in her room. So, I went downstairs to get Uncle Will, but he was gone too. We were all alone. And Ryan screaming real bad. Now, there was this stuff my mother called pain killer she kept in her room. An I got it, and gave Ryan a big spoonful. He said it helped, so I gave him more. Then, he fell asleep. An I went downstairs and sat on the front steps to wait. It was still summer and real hot. All morning I sat there. Once or twice I heard cows bawling from the barn, but I didn't go feed 'em. I was scared. Didn't know why, exactly, just scared. Couple a times I went up to check on Ryan, but he was still sleepin'. Well, on about four o'clock, Uncle Will came back. An he had a woman in the car with him, but I saw right away she weren't my mother. "You and your brother get your stuff together." says Uncle Will. "You're going with this lady." "Where's my mother?" I said. "Gone," he says. "Up and run away." An he walks past me into the house. The Aid Lady went right up to see Ryan soon as I said he was sick, and I followed Uncle Will into the kitchen. "Yer lyin'." I says to him. He just looks at me. "Yer mother was a bad lot." he says. "And you'll be another. Wild little brat." Boy was I mad. I screamed at him. "My mother wouldn't leave us—you made her—you made her go!" I was just about to run at him, fists an all, when the Aid Lady comes running down the stairs so fast she practically falls into the kitchen—"Get a doctor, get a doctor!" she's yellin'. Then she grabs me and starts shaking me and asking questions so fast I don't have time to answer. "What have you done? What have you and your mother done to that poor boy?" I was cryin', but I told her how Ryan had this pain, and how I gave him the medicine called pain killer, and how he just went to sleep ... Finally, she lets me go. "And we're not going with you." I said. "Ryan an me are going with my mother." Aid Lady looks kinda tired now. "You'll go where you're told." she says. "You've got nobody now. Your brother is dead."(*a beat*) They never told me, you know, if it was on account of what I give him, or 'cause he was so sick. Saw these pearls in Eaton's once, knew my mother would have stopped to look at them—an this red wool coat, real warm. I dress her up all the time in my mind ... all the time.

Available from Playwrights Union of Canada as a copyscript.

BEAUX GESTES ET BEAUTIFUL DEEDS

by Marie-Lynn Hammond

A young woman seeks to resolve her split identity by uncovering the truth about her grandmothers. One is a rich, flamboyant WASP, the other a poor, hardworking French-Canadian with a survivor's sense of humour. Elsie is the Anglophone grandmother.

2:50

ELSIE

It wasn't just my running away of course, or even running away with a flyer. No. What people found really galling was the fact that I myself had decided to learn to fly. And flying was about the last thing someone of my position was expected to take up. Women had barely earned the right to smoke in public, let alone fly. Back then, flying was adventurous, glamorous too, but also considered rather—how shall we say—bohemian? Well, it was the flyers you see. They swaggered. They drank. They wore silk scarves and wonderful boots. They were—oh let's face it they were damned sexy, and that was the problem. Still, that day, when I saw the pilot fly under the bridge, I didn't care a fig for what anyone thought. I'd made up my mind to learn and that was that. Shortly after though, the war ended. Douglas came home, I became pregnant and had a baby instead. Arthur Barnard. Barney. A lovely baby; all dark curls and blue eyes. For a while I thought he'd be enough. But then one evening, Douglas and I went to a party. It was rather a dull affair, and I'd already caused a flap simply by showing up in a cerise-coloured dress; but I had the devil in me that night, so at one point I said quite loudly: "By the way Douglas, did I mention that I've decided to learn to fly?" There was dead silence for a moment, then the men began to snort and chuckle; "Hey Elsie," laughed one of them, "in that case you ought to meet Lieutenant Dobbin here. He's a flyer." Douglas later accused me of flirting, but I swear I wasn't, because at first glance this fellow Dobbin wasn't my type at all. He was short, almost stocky, with a rough and ready manner and an insolent grin. "Pleased to meet you, Mrs. Hammond. I've been admiring your outfit. It isn't everyone that can carry something like that off." "Why, thank you. I'm afraid we women must seek adventure in whatever small ways are open to us." "Listen, are you serious about this flying business? It's dangerous—a lot more dangerous than wearing a red dress." "I don't care. I think flying is the most marvellous thing on earth!" Then I told him about the pilot I'd seen flying at the Victory rally. "Well," he said, grinning, "Under the bridge you say? That was none other than myself." "I don't believe you! You're just like all the other men here, you don't take me seriously at all." Then he stopped smiling and looked me straight in the eye: "On the contrary, I take you very seriously. In fact, I'm going to make you an offer. Some fellows and me, we've bought a couple of Curtiss Jennies, and we keep 'em out near Brown's Pasture. If you want to come out someday, I'll take you up for a ride. And if you still want to learn to fly after that, I'll teach you." Well, I was thrilled! The next day Ted just turned up out of the blue, took me by the arm and said "Come along Elsie—today I'm giving you your first flying lesson." And I should have learned then, shouldn't I? But I didn't. Why? Because I made the mistake of falling in love with my instructor. And once you fall in love with a man, they'll never teach you anything. First they get critical, then they lose their patience, and finally, they become so insulting that you're scared they won't love you anymore and you cry out, "Stop! You're right. I'm slow, I'm stupid, and we needn't do this again, ever! Now let's go and have a drink at the Chateau, please!" Then they take you in their arms and murmur, "Darling, I didn't mean to be hard on you. I just hate to see you wasting your time, that's all!" Men. Well it doesn't matter. What matters is that Ted loved me and I loved him. Besides, I went with him on countless flights, and saw the world in ways I could never have imagined. Sometimes he'd let me take the controls—swearing of course that we'd all be killed—but planes were a lot simpler in those days, and I did just fine. So I never did get my license. I never did fly solo. Because once I was with Ted, I didn't care to anymore ... I mean, why go alone when you can go together? Never did fly solo. But really, I've ... no regrets.

Available from Playwrights Union of Canada as a copyscript.

s 200 words is indeed short, and there isn't one single anecdote that typifies the audition experience, I thought I'd jot down a list of suggested "don'ts" for actors to consider. I've experienced all of these, and hope that publishing them here will help me to never experience them again.

1) Don't hit the auditioner

2) Don't use a banana as a prop - it's very crude.

3) Don't spend all your appointment time getting into character.

4) Don't spend any time at all getting into character if there isn't going to be an appreciable difference.

5) Don't use more than 30 props. It takes too long to set them up.

6) Don't admit you heard about the audition yesterday and were memorizing your "speech" on the bus down.

7) Don't eat your lunch during your appointment. It's not very interesting.

Admittedly this betrays a certain negativity towards the audition experience that I don't entirely subscribe to. I've enjoyed a great many auditions, but thought this would prove more useful. And trust me, I have my own list of things directors shouldn't do.

Paul Mears
Artistic Director
The New Play Centre
Vancouver, B.C.

Next?

**ENTLEMEN**

Audition, noun, awd-ish-on, the act or faculty of hearing; a performance (esp. for stage, broadcasting, etc.) as a test of competency (Latin, auditio, a hearing)

1. *Probably apocryphal* - an actress who had the reputation for always demanding the last word, was auditioning for the role of Mrs. Alving in Ibsen's GHOSTS. In rehearsal she was faithful to the text, but at the audition it went thus:

Oswald: Give me the sun, Mother.
Mrs. Alving: No!

2.   *Not apocryphal* - an actor of some repute arrived to audition for a role in Brecht's MOTHER COURAGE. He spent an inordinate amount of time preparing and getting into the mood of the piece centre stage, and when the stage manager informed him they were ready to hear him, the actor stepped forward with all the confidence in the world and said: "I'm leaving for the thirty years' war" - and left.

3.   The late Richard Rodgers and Oscar Hammerstein II were dutifully impressed with a young lady auditioning for one of their Broadway musicals. She belted out her song with considerable style and panache, and by the sixteenth bar was obviously a natural contender for the role - anyway it went like this:Auditionee:

> You say tomatoe   Tomatoe - tomahtoe
> And I say tomahtoe   Potato - potahto
> You say potato   Let's call the whole thing off
> And I say potahto

Mr. Rodgers: Thank you Miss Levine.
To which she replied - LEVENE!

Tom Kneebone
Artistic Director
Smile Theatre Company
Toronto, Ontario

ONE THOUSAND CRANES

by Colin Thomas

A 12-year-old Canadian boy tries to cope with his fear of nuclear war and a young Japanese survivor of the A-Bomb discovers she has leukemia. This powerful drama celebrates hope and peace for the future.

1:05

BUDDY

The end of the world? Oh, snap! I've gotta tell you. It was so weird. I was in the mall? ... and this crazy guy, he walks right up to me and he starts screaming, "Are you ready for the end of the world?" And I just stand there. I mean, what am I supposed to do? And then he takes off. Feeow! Like he's being chased by the police from the planet Bazonkers. And then I went into the stereo store and all these TV's in the store were showing this guy and there's been an accident in this nuclear reactor. And this guy looks awful—all burned up and everything. And then all of a sudden all of these TV's, all hundred and seventy million of them, they zoom in on this one guy, real close, and I look into his eyes, and ... it's like I'm in the TV's! I feel like I am that guy! And I can feel my body, like what his body feels like. And it's burning! Like my body was burning up, I felt like I was gonna throw up, I felt like I was gonna die! And then a commercial comes on and I'm saved. Ooohohoho. Isn't that weird? It made me think about ... the end of the world ... you know ... the real end of the world ... like nuclear war.

Published by Simon & Pierre Publishing Co. Ltd.—trade paperback.

DR. BARNARDO'S PIONEERS

by Rick McNair

*An episodic treatment of the Barnardo Children, youngsters
sent from the slums of England to homes—some good, some
bad—in Canada.*

1:25

JIM

I ain't got no mother. Ain't got no father.

I didn't have any friends. I didn't live anywhere. The streets was me
home. I lived with a bunch of boys down near Wopping Way. I did
odd jobs with a boatman, to help him on his barge. He treated me
very bad. Knocked me about somethin' frightful. He used to beat
me for nothing and sometimes I didn't have nothin' to eat for days.
Sometimes, for fun, he'd set the dog on me and he chewed me up
somethin' frightful. Finally I couldn't take it no more and I runned
away. I thought I were going to be happy now, 'specially as most
people took pity on me and give me a penny now and then. But lor,
sir, the police were the worse; they always kept a-movin' me on.
Twice I were up before the magistrate for sleepin' out. When the
bobbies catched me, sometimes, they'd let me off with a kick or a
good knock on the side of the 'ead. But one night an awful cross
fellow caught me sleepin' on a doorstep an' locked me up. Then I
got six days at the workhouse, an' afterwards runned away; an' ever
since I've been in and out, up an' down where I could. I ain't had no
luck at all, an' it's been sleepin' out on an empty stomach almost
every night.

Then Barnardo asked me if there were more boys like me in London.
Oh yes, sir, lots ... 'eaps of 'em; more than I could count. So he
asked me to take him to where some of them poor boys were and I
told him. That oi will, sir. I did too.

———

Published by NeWest Press—trade paperback.

RATTLE IN THE DASH

by Peter Anderson

A cross-country car trip in pursuit of a woman turns in to something quite unexpected.

1:00

BRANDON

I ever tell you about the time my old man ran into our house? I was five or six and I was upstairs in bed and my mother was reading me this bedtime story when we hear this crash, sounds like thunder only it come from downstairs. My mother tells me to stay in bed and goes down to see what's up. She doesn't come back for a while so I tiptoe down the stairs and right there in the living room is the old man's Thunderbird. It's half inside and half outside and there's bricks all over and this perfect half-circle knocked out of the wall. And there's the T-Bird sitting in the middle of the living room with the stars shining through. And this big crowd of neighbours in pyjamas and housecoats standing around outside staring into our house. Nobody was talking. They were staring in at me and my mom and the T-Bird in the living room. My old man was sitting there behind the steering wheel with this stunned kind of look on his face like he couldn't believe it. I thought it was the most terrific thing he'd ever done.

———

Published by Playwrights Canada Press—trade paperback.

SKIN

by Dennis Foon

Teenagers from diverse cultural backgrounds experience racism in the education system.

1:20

TUAN

Sometimes late at night when I am mopping floors, I stop and listen. The empty building, so hollow. Buzzing of fluorescent tubes. Outside rain beats against windows. I feel ... like I'm underwater. I think: around the corner, my older brother will be standing. Waiting to grab the mop from my hands, shouting, "You're my little brother, why are you working when you should be sleeping? Give that mop to me, that is my job!" And I look at him, and his hair is still wet, wet like it was the last time I saw him. I want to say, "Did you swim, I thought you drowned. How did you find me here, in Canada, in this city, in this building right now? You didn't drown, you're alive and you made it all the way to me." ... and I walk down the corridor, turn the corner and look. The hallway goes on forever. It's so empty. No sound but the hum of lights. And the rain against the windows.

When I found out Lo was dead, it was such a puzzle. Why should I live and Lo die? We were so much the same—why not me? I remember he always said that I was a survivor. He'd laugh, tease me ... now I just wish he was a survivor too. By next year I will have enough money to bring my parents here. I'm glad they will be safe. They are very excited but as for me, I don't want to think about the future. For me, it is as hard to look forward as it is to look back. So I live for today. For each moment. And live as best I can.

Published in "Skin & Liars" by Playwrights Canada Press—trade paperback.

I do have another, little something I've been working on.

WELCOME TO THE NHL

by Alan Williams

A warm, comic look at the facts, faults, foibles and fallacies of Canada's character and its national sport.

3:30

TONY

I first came to Canada in 1972. I was ten, and I had been raised on the banks of the Nile, in Uganda. Then Idi Amin shot my dad, so I was sent to Canada to stay with my mother's cousin. This was south-western Manitoba. Pretty different! Nobody knew how to talk to me. Every so often someone would say something like, "So! The Nile eh?," and I'd say, "Yes," and they'd say, "Hmmm ... the Nile. Well that's different!" and that was that. After about three weeks, Uncle Jack, my foster father, said, "Want to see where all the excitement in town is?" I said, "Yes." He took me to a big hut with a lot of people in it. They all stood up and said: "I pledge: My head to clearer thinking, My heart to greater loyalty, My health to better living, and My hands to greater services, For my club, my community and my country." Cold chills went through me. I thought, "It's a political society!" This was the 4-H Beef Club Achievement Night. All it was was kids getting prizes for their pet cattle. I'm looking at Uncle Jack, and I'm thinking, "So this is where all the excitement in town is, eh? Bunch of fat kids walking around with cows?" I started to pity myself. I started to think that no one was telling me what was going on. What got people excited here. I got depressed. I went on a code of silence. I sat around and watched T.V. all the time.

Then one night, Uncle Jack and some of his friends came to watch with me. I thought, "What's this? Is this something that gets them excited?"

Hard to tell ... it was just a bunch of guys with sticks running around on ice. Bunch of guys from Russia, and a bunch of guys from Canada. But they all came back a few days later, and watched it again. I couldn't figure out whether they were interested or not. And then at the end of one session ... I thought, "This is it!" But it was hard to tell how they felt. They came back a few more times, and then ... (*as if he was two hockey fans watching a game on television*)

"Well, they sure took their time."

"Yup."

I just didn't get it! Were they bothered! But at least it was a clue. So when they asked me what I wanted to do, I said to my step-parents, "I want to learn hockey." "Wait till it gets cold," they said. And it did. So when the place freezed up for the first time ...

One November morning they got me up before dawn, dressed me up, and drove me to the outside rink. About two months after this my mother turned up and took me to live in Toronto, where we kind of slipped into the African community, and I never played hockey again. But in those last two months, everyone was friendly. Even people who had not been at the game would smile and say, "Hi, Tretiak." This year I found myself close by and went to visit the rink, for the first time. Oscar was still there—after sixteen years! I said, "Do you still remember me?" He said "Sure! You're the one that knocked over that goon coach, Fraser. Stood up to the little dictator. He was never the same again." "Do you remember my name?" I asked. "Tretiak," he said, "the little freedom fighter." This is ridiculous. All I remember was feeling ashamed for having lost my temper. But he didn't seem to understand that. I read there was a Canadian explorer, who walked up to the Arctic and back. When they asked him what he wanted for his epitaph he said, "I know how I felt when I did it." This is how I feel. I am glad I played hockey because I know how I felt when I did it.

Published by Blizzard Publishing Ltd.—trade paperback.

URBAN VOODOO

by Jim Millan & Peter Hinton

Grisly urban myths woven with daily life in this bizarre tale of the Blaine family.

1:35

BUZZ

Like ya know how we got this house? On my 5th birthday, my mom
organized a party for me with all of my little friends. They all piled
into the McDonald's station wagon. Mrs. McDonald was gonna
help mind the kids at the restaurant so Mom didn't have to manage
by herself. Marc and Buster all dressed nice. Sat with Mommy in
the front seat. Mommy all smiles. Everyone all perfectly behaved.
We got to Scott's Chicken Villa near the highway and pile out and
go into the party. They're expecting us, of course, and have little
hats and plastic Colonel Sanders piggy banks. Gross girls in nylon
outfits. It's all the same in those places. So they start bringing out
the dinner on little paper plates. One piece of chicken each, with
one scoop of macaroni salad. They plop mine down in front of me
and give Marc and my best friend Jerry ours first because I'm the
Birthday Boy. Mom says to wait for everyone so I start lookin' at it.
I had a big piece of chicken, but it didn't look like a breast or
anything, so I poked at it with my fork but the plastic fork doesn't
go in. I push harder with the fork as the girl gives out the last plates
of food. I push with the fork and the chicken rolls over, and the little
pink feet and tail pop out. I start screamin. The girl drops the last
two plates and they knock over the drinks, and roll the "Kentucky
Fried Rat" at my mom. She sees this thing moving and smashes at it
with her hand. And it goes flying at the girl. The girl starts
screamin, this really high-pitched scream and Mrs. McDonald starts
gaggin like she's gonna choke. Like she's gonna throw up or
somethin. Mom starts grabbin Marc and says, "We're going,
children we're getting out." And all the kids are sobbing and
covered in Coke. And slidin out of the booth over the food and all

- 144 -

stare at the dead rat on the floor and this sobbin redhead girl. It was like a movie, this whole thing. Anyways, Mom sued and Scott's Chicken Villa gave $125,000 not to speak to the press. We paid off the mortgage, and still get interest off the 75 Gs we got left. And that's enough to get by, with Dad's pension.

––––––––

Available from Playwrights Union of Canada as a copyscript.

CORNELIUS DRAGON

by Jan Truss

A contemporary prairie immigrant boy on the verge of an uncomfortable adolescence runs away and hunts for the inner courage he needs.

2:00

CORNELIUS

There was this dance, see. A carnival dance with funny hats. Everybody dressed nice. I'd put this stuff on my face to hide my spots. Washed my hair. Got a new shirt. My dad let me buy a shirt. I was glad. The shirts my dad made were always different. I hated them—because they were different. Didn't like to tell my dad about his shirts. Anyhow, I'd got a new shirt like everybody else's. Deodorant. Aftershave, everything—the lot. Tonight I was going to ask Kathy to dance.

I could see her across there in the crowd with her hair all shiny. And a new dress that was soft so you couldn't help looking right at her figure, you know. Wow, she was pretty, laughing, happy, talking to everybody. Tonight—I was going to ask her. Tonight—I had to do it. I'd promised myself. There was no backing down.

I looked at her talking to Larry Thomas. Waving her hands as she talked. Larry Thomas who got A's in everything. Did everything. Did everybody—he said.

Anyhow, I was going to ask her.

I started to walk across the auditorium floor. It seemed like everybody was on the other side. And everybody was watching me. What if I fell over on the slippery stuff they put on the floor?

Is my fly undone? Does the stuff on my spots show? Are my pants too tight? Nicked in someplace? Or not tight enough? Baggy? Bet I've gone all red. Crazy hat. Should I take it off? No. Everybody else's wearing crazy hats. Pretend you don't care—so what! Everybody's laughing. Feels like they're all laughing at me. Staring at me. Except Kathy. She's pretending she hasn't seen me coming. But I can't stop now. Touch her to make her look. Gee—she smells nice. Everything goes quiet. Everybody's listening. "Kathy. Kathy, wantodance?" My voice like a shout in silence. Everybody hears. I have to say it again. "Kathy, wantodance?" She stops what she's saying to Larry Thomas. She gives me one sick look and she steps back.

"You've got to be kidding," she says ... "You've got to be kidding." And Larry Thomas laughs. And she laughs. And everybody bursts out laughing. You've got to be kidding. You've got to be kidding.

Published in "Eight Plays for Young People" by NeWest Press—a trade paperback.

DREAMING AND DUELLING

by John Lazarus and Joa Lazarus

Fantasies and love for the same girl lead two fencing students to "play" with the safety tips off and the points sharpened. A look at adolescent role-playing.

1:45

ERIC

You got to promise never to tell anybody. And don't interrupt. If you screw around with this, I'll kill you. (*pausing*) I was really upset even before the funeral. 'Cause I'd read about what they do to the carcass, how they drain out the blood and put in embalming fluid, whatever that is. And they put makeup on their face. So already I was pissed off. And in the car on the way there everybody was sobbing and snorting and wailing about what a great guy he was. That killed me. Nobody ever told him that when he was alive. When it might have done him some good. No, they saved it up 'til he killed himself, and then they all told each other.

So I was really steamed when we got there. And we went in, and I knew he would have makeup on, but I wasn't ready for what he looked like. I almost didn't recognize him. He looked so beautiful. Like pretty. He looked like a woman.

And then, during the eulogy—you know what the minister did in the middle of the eulogy? Checked his watch. He checked his wristwatch. This guy baptized me, right, he was in charge of our youth group, I always thought he was God's personal best friend. And I look at him and he seems like just this jowly old businessman checking his watch while he's making a cheap speech.

And then, as we're filing out at the end, my mother tells me I should kiss my father for the very last time. Very last time, I love that, I'd never kissed him since—grade one. And I leaned over him, and he really smelled good. I expected some kind of chemical smell, but he smelled so nice. So I kissed him. And he wasn't chilly or stiff or anything, it felt like he could have been alive. And—I suddenly realized—look, I think I told you enough. (*pausing*) I realized I was getting this—I already had this really enormous hard-on, if you laugh I'll tear you to bits, you tell anybody this and I'll kill you, I had this huge rod, and I pulled away from him real fast and looked around. And my mother had this sly, kind of sexy look on her face like she'd caught me at it and she thought it was funny. And I looked at the minister. And boy, the look on *his* face. Like he was ready to send me straight to Hell. And I wanted to say, "I loved the guy, at least I loved him. What did you do? You checked your damn watch!" But I didn't say anything. But that's when I quit the Church, man, that moment. If that's the best they can come up with when somebody dies, forget it. And if you laugh, I'll slaughter you.

Available from Playwrights Union of Canada as a copyscript.

SALT-WATER MOON

by David French

On a moonlit night in 1926, Jacob Mercer returns home to Coley's Point to try and win back the heart of 17-year-old Mary Snow. This is a love story full of humour, poetry, and all the magic of a starry Newfoundland evening. Winner, 1985 Drama Award, Canadian Authors' Association.

1:30

JACOB

Yes, and all Will McKenzie could do was wait for a brave man to march home so's he could whittle him down to size seven years later. The same man who was part of the famous Blue Puttees, same as your own father. The same man who crawled t'rough the trenches at Gallipoli in 1915 in his tropical fit-out, twenty-seven days on the firing line without taking off a stitch or having a wash. The same man who endured the November storm they called the worst in forty years, with two hundred men swept away in the flooded trenches or frozen to death when the rains stopped and the killing frost set in. Rubbing their feet with whale oil and stuffing 'em into sandbags filled with straw … He'd sit in the mud at Suvla Plain and try to eat a piece of bread and jam, and the flies that t'ick the bread would be black before he could get it to his mouth—the same flies that bred in the corpses in No Man's Land. He still wakes up in a sweat, Mother says. Rats are crawling over him, the way they done in the trenches in France. Rats bigger than cats snapping at his boots and stepping over his face in the dark, their whiskers tickling his ears … But the worst of the dreams always start the same way: with the women in black ploughing the fields, no more than the fling of a stone from that tiny French village, July 1, 1916. The day he faced the German guns and lived, lying wounded in No Man's Land, with that tin triangle of the 29th Division on his back—a piece of metal cut from a biscuit tin and painted red. He couldn't move an inch or the tin would glint in the sun and the snipers would pick him off. So he lay there under that blazing sun of July till dark came, pressing his pain into the bloodied earth beneath him. One of the men the Germans called the 'White Savages'. And this is the same man, Mary, that was under the t'umb of Jerome's father last summer and had to do what he was told, the law being the law, Military Medal or no!

Published by Talon Books—trade paperback.

s a director who has somewhat of a tin ear—well, you don't want to hear me sing—doing THREEPENNY OPERA was an exciting challenge.

Auditionees were in abundance. After all, Touchstone Theatre primarily produces new Canadian works—casting a musical that everyone who has seen the McDonald's commercial is familiar with brought forward many potential self-professed Lotte Lenyas.

My favourite was a young lady who admitted when booking an appointment that she really wasn't a singer but could sure sell a song. Why she then chose to prepare a rousing a cappella version of "Doe, a deer—a female deer …" I'll never know. Even I could tell by the first three 'notes' that we were in big trouble. To her credit, she did have the *Absolute Undivided Attention* of myself, the musical director, the choreographer, the stage manager and the assistant director. We didn't dare look away and certainly not at each other. The second verse, where she was really going for it, was accompanied by a kind of chicken dance that may have been the last word in Brecht's alienation technique. Despite this unique performance, I'm afraid we didn't call her back—in fact, I believe we needed an unscheduled fifteen-minute break to recover.

Roy Surette
Artistic Director
Touchstone Theatre
Vancouver, B.C.

QUIET IN THE LAND

by Anne Chislett

Yock brings about a crisis in his Amish community by fighting in the First World War. Winner of the 1982 Chalmers Canadian Play Award and the 1983 Governor General's Award.

1:30

YOCK

Pa, I have to talk to you ... I have to. Open the door. Open it! I been half way 'round the world and I've come back. I've come to tell you something and you're going to listen. You never listened to me in your life, did you? Well, listen now. I killed a man. Do you hear me, Pa? I killed a man. They tell me I killed more, but there was only one I ever saw. We were going up this hill and he came at me. I stuck out my bayonet like it was my arm, and I got him in the gut. He was lying in the mud, screaming and bleeding. Everybody else kept going on, but I just stood there shaking. He was going to die right there in that mud and he knew it. He was afraid, Pa. He was afraid of facing God. He started screaming for a preacher. I wanted to tell him I understood, that I was Christian, that I was German too. I wanted to say all those words I used to hear you read from the Bible, but I was ashamed. So I let him die like that in the mud. That was the war, Pa. That's what it was. You know, I thought I was going off to save you all from something. I bet he did, too. I thought the King of England was going to be there like in the school books, cheering me on. Somehow I even thought I was going to put the legs back on Paddy O'Rourke. But all I did was put a knife into a man ... and Pa, he looked like Zepp. If he'd had a beard, he could have been Zepp. And right at the end, he cried out for his father to come and take him home, and I started crying for you. I wanted you to come over the hill and take me home. Because I knew, if I'd just stayed home ... I guess that's what I ... what I wanted to tell you, Pa ... If I'd just stayed. I'm going away now. You don't have to worry. I'll keep out of your way ...

Published by Coach House Press—trade paperback.

CREEPS

by David Freeman

Stealing time in a washroom from their jobs in a sheltered workshop, four cerebral palsy victims spit out their frustrations and, reluctantly, their dreams. They talk about sex, personalities, scandal and despair while their welfare supervisor pounds on the door. Winner, 1972 Chalmers Canadian Play Award, New York Drama Desk Award and three Distinguished Achievement Awards from the LA Drama Critics Circle.

1:25

PETE

When I came to this dump eleven years ago, I wanted to be a carpenter. That's all I could think about ever since I can remember. But face it, whoever heard of a carpenter with a flipper like that? (*holding up his deformed hand*) But I had a nice chat with this doc and he told me I'd find what I'm looking for down here. So I came down here, and one of Saunders' flunkies shoves a bag of blocks in my hand. "What gives?" I said. And then it slowly dawned on me that as far as the doc is concerned, that's the closest I'll ever get to carpentry.

And I was pissed off, sure. But then I think, good old doc, he just doesn't understand me. 'Cause I still have my ideals. So in a few days I bust out of this place and go looking for a job—preferably carpentry. What happens? I get nothing but aching feet and a flat nose from having fucking doors slammed in my face all the fucking time.

And I'm at my wits' end when I get a letter from the Spastic Club. And I said fuck that. I'm about to throw it in the furnace, but I get curious. I've heard of the Spastic Club and I always figured it was a load of shit. But I think one meeting isn't going to kill me.

So I go, and I find out I'm right. It's a load of shit. It's a bunch of fuckheads sitting around saying, "Aren't we just too ducky for these poor unfortunate cripples?" But I got a free turkey dinner.

When I got home I took a good look at myself. I ask myself what am I supposed to be fighting? What do these jokers want me to do? The answer is they want to make life easier for me. Is that so bad? I mean, they don't expect me to keep you guys in your place or nothing. They just want me to enjoy life. And the government even pays me just for doing that. If I got a job, I'd lose the pension. So why have I been breaking my ass all this time looking for a job? And I got no answers to that. So I take the pension, and come back to the workshop. The only price I gotta pay is listening to old lady Saunders giving me hell for not weaving her goddamn rug.

Available in: Modern Canadian Drama published by Penguin Books Canada—trade paperback; Modern Canadian Plays published by Talon Books; Reprinted with kind permission of J.C. Goodwin and Associates.

SISTER JUDE

by Dave Carley

Wesley, in his mid-twenties, is engaged in a mighty wrestling match with his personal demons. He has climbed the highest point in his town and stands with coathangers in both hands, arms raised, inviting the wrath of God in an electrical storm.

2:30

WESLEY

(*muttering*) Rain. Come on rain. More lightning. (*looking up*) Make it rain hard. (*pausing*) More electricity! Good. I have to tell you this out loud. This hill is as close as I can get to you. There's nothing between us God. It's just me, then sky, then you. So show me what to do. (*seeing lightning*) That's good.

Forgive me for I have sinned. I have sinned repeatedly and with ingenuity. I have gone out of my way to sin. I have slow-danced with the Devil.

Every Friday since my late teens I have put buttons the size of dimes in Globe and Mail honour boxes and then I have removed not one but two papers so that Mom and I could do the Jumbo Crosswords separately. I told her I paid for the Globes out of my own pocket and I have knowingly accepted her gratitude.

There's worse.

(*rapidly*) I broke the Crown Derby gravy boat accidentally and then begged Jude to glue it back up before Mom could see. I crumpled somebody's bumper in the K-Mart parking lot and I didn't leave a note on their windshield. I have drunk Shooting Sherry to excess. (*pausing*) Seven times. I have never smoked a cigarette but I have wanted to. OH GOD OH GOD OH GOD I lie even to you. I *have* smoked a cigarette! I found it on the street and I lit it—knew how from watching Jude—I lit it and then I walked down Monroe Avenue and I felt ... virile.

There's worse.

- 156 -

I come up here often. I come up here on Armour Hill every night there's no moon. This is where Jude and Billy used to come and park. I saw them here. Once. Twice. More than that. Many more times. I saw them and I saw others. This is where everyone else from school comes to park and pet and feel and fornicate and I came up here too—I still come up here—and I sneak from car to car and I look in the windows, sometimes they're too steamy to see anything but God it's true and I do this night after night after night. I don't want to do it! I just do it!

I *like* doing it! I don't want to like doing it but I do and I can't stop! (*raising coathangers in each hand*) Now you know it all.
Everything I do and everything I think. They aren't the thoughts and actions of a worthy man, are they. (*raising arms higher*) You've got to let me know. You've got to send me a sign.

(*throwing his arms high*) STRIKE ME DOWN OH MIGHTY HEAVENLY FATHER STRIKE ME DOWN WITH A BOLT OF LIGHTNING I DON'T HAVE RUBBER-SOLED SHOES ON HIT ME HIT ME HIT ME I AM THE WILLING VESSEL OF YOUR WRATH HIT ME HIT ME HIT ME … Strike me down … smite me … (*pausing; lowering arms slowly; joy in face and voice*) Why haven't you … struck … me down …

Am I a worthy man?

Are my sins forgiven?

Hallelujah.

Available from Playwrights Union of Canada as a copyscript.

GOOSE SPIT

by Vivienne Laxdal

A group of young Vancouver Island locals come to terms with their future as the early '80's brings them sex, drugs, rock 'n roll and unemployment.

1:25

BEN

This is really fucked up, you know? Over two years it's been. For the first time since then I think I might be interested in another lady and, at the same time, Sandy's face keeps popping into my brain, stronger than ever. It's like the closer I get to Gail, the harder I gotta work at forgetting Sandy. You'd think it would be easier.

On the way up to Stokum she said this time she was going to jump. She never had the guts before that. Just watching us jump the falls scared her to bits. But this time ... I remember, she promised. She was going to jump.

Jesus, we were high that day. On top of the world. Remember how hot it was? Even the water wasn't bad. Didn't turn you blue like usual. And it was really bright out. The sun was right over our heads ... and the water was all shimmering. It was like a mirror, shining the sun back in our eyes.

When we climbed up ... I never saw those kids playing on the log down there. They must've pushed it in from the side ... and up top, the sun was so bright, like I said, so we couldn't see straight down. The water's so loud there, you can never hear anything ... not really.

When we got up top, she chickened out again. I thought I'd help her. I mean, once you done it the first time, it's easy, right? You just gotta do that first jump. Sometimes, you need an extra little ... push.

I never saw that log, or those kids. She screamed. But just like it was fun ... I was just helping. Helping her take that first jump.

Available from Playwrights Union of Canada as a copyscript.

WILD ABANDON

by Daniel MacIvor

A young man's dark, humorous and static observations about life, the universe and his real mother.

1:25

STEVE

One time? I was a little kid like nine—this woman? We were out in some stupid family rest-o-rant and everybody's fighting in low voices and complaining about the food and that, and this woman, sitting over across at another table, she keeps looking at me, staring at me. I don't say nothing and I start thinking: she's really staring okay! and I start thinking: "Hey! This woman, she's my real mother right. She followed me here. She's been watching me for weeks and she's my real mother and she's gonna come over and say "This boy is my son" and take me away from my stupid ugly family who won't let me do nothing and never let me talk and never let me listen and won't let me have a black room. She'd take me away and out into her new car—that smells new and—a convertible and—with the roof down and we'd drive far away to this house—this castle she lives in and I'd live there too and I'd have my own huge fucking room ... So I'm thinking this and the woman, she gets up and starts walking over to me. I'm thinking: "HOLY SHIT! HOLY SHIT! It really IS my mother!" I got so nervous. She comes right up to me. Standing right there. I'm sitting down okay, she's right there, and she reaches back ... and jabs this fork into my stomach and starts screaming: "DEVIL'S EYES DEVIL'S EYES DEVIL'S EYES!"

Published by Playwrights Canada Press—trade paperback.

THE CRACKWALKER

by Judith Thompson

*This remarkable play about a retarded woman and her
friends explores the psyche of those living outside of
"normal" society.*

1:30

JOE

Martin—Martin wasn't an asshole, but he was stupid you know?
Jeez he was stupid. So this Friday night we'd all gotten pissed up
the Manor, eh, then we all went over to the island just to fuck
around and to see the Mayor's sister, Linda, who was workin at the
General Wolfe waitin on tables. So Bart, that was his real name,
Bart and me and Martin had all got these new boots over at the A-1
men's store, really nice you know, all leather, real solid a hundred
bucks a pair so we wanted to show em off to Linda, you know, bug
her. So Bart gets in there and he's jumpin on tables, eatin all the
limes and cherries and that for the drinks singin some gross song
about his love boots, he called them. Fuck it was funny—we were
killin ourselves but Linda she wasn't laughin her boss was gettin
pissed off so she told Bart, she goes "Bart, get the fuck out of here I
think your goddamn boots are shit." That's what she said. So he
give her a big kiss right in front of her boss and we take off in
Martin's car. Me and the Mayor in the backseat, Martin and his
girlfriend in the front. Well we're headin down the road goin south
it's dark but it ain't wet and the last thing I remember Bart looks at
me and he says "I wonder what it's like to fuck an angel" and bang
everything goes fuckin black. When I come to I'm in the fucking
ambulance goin across to Kingston and Bart's lying there beside me
dead only I didn't know it and there's his sister Linda right there in
the ambulance. I don't know how she got there—she's all red all
black under her eyes and that and she's bawlin just bawlin up a
storm and she's huggin his legs and she's sayin something only I
can't make out what she's sayin I can't make it out I was so out of it

I'm thinkin I'm gonna die I'm thinkin I'm gonna die if I don't make out what she's sayin so I kept tryin to make it out and she kept sayin it and then I knew what she was sayin and you know what it was? ... She was sayin she did like his boots. "I do like your boots Bart I do like your boots Bart I do like your boots I do like your fuckin boots I do like your boots I do like your boots I do like your boots." (*fading out*) ... She wouldn't fuckin stop it.

———

Published in "The Other Side of the Dark" by Coach House Press—trade paperback.

WILD ABANDON

by Daniel MacIvor

*A young man's dark, humorous and static observations
about life, the universe and his real mother.*

2:35

STEVE

I go to this diner.
Not a rest-o-rant I hate rest-o-rants I never go to rest-o-rants I only
go to diners. And I only go to diners that have all-day breakfasts
because who the hell are they to tell me when I should eat
breakfast? Who the hell are they to tell me when I should get out of
bed? This particular breakfast this particular day was three, four
o'clock. Sausages, hash browns, WHITE toast, BLACK coffee and
eggs over EASY! Very easy, so you can still taste the rawness in the
yolk; so you can almost ... taste ... that ... chicken.
Sometimes jam sometimes not depends on the day this day no. So
I'm sitting there looking out the window thinking about how when
trees are dead and the leaves are gone you can see so much more of
the world and this woman four, four and half feet away left side
starts taking to her friend in this pretty loud voice about this trip she
took to Mexico.
"There were so many Gringos."
Yeah. I'm serious. Gringos. That's what she said. And then? Every
time the guy brings something over to the table she goes "Gracias!"
Gracias like she took one trip there and she turns into fucking
Mexico. But that be okay, but that be okay until she starts talking
about being on this bus with all these "Men" and she says "Men"
like it's some kind of disease or a new drug. "Men."
And what am I? I'm a man. I'm a man sitting right there.
She'd be looking right at me if she'd just turn her head this much.
She practically is staring at me without even moving her eyes at all.
I'm right there!
Then! Out of nowhere, she's telling her friend about the Grand

Canyon. The fucking Grand Canyon's not in Mexico!

What am I supposed to think right?

THEN! Fuck ... Then she's describing this dream she had where all
the "Men" are growing out of the walls in her apartment. All these
"Men." So I was pretty fed up right—

And not because she's a woman, don't think that okay I got nothing
against women—Fake mothers I do! Fake mothers who come up to
you in rest-o-rants and stab you in the guts with a fork I do! But this
woman here it was just her Person-Ality that was pissing me off ...
and how she was saying all this shit just so somebody would hear
her. I'm sitting right there!

So.

So I lean over and I say: "Excuse me. Why don't you go get some
help!" Yeah I did.

No I didn't.

I didn't say that. What I said was: "If you want to sleep with me
why don't you just say so?"

No I didn't.

I didn't say nothing. (*pausing*)

But you know what I did do though?

I got up, and I changed my seat!

That's almost as good as saying something.

And I never went back to that diner either.

Not because of her ... but because they got my fucking eggs wrong!

———————

*Published in "See Bob Run & Wild Abandon" by Playwrights Canada
Press—trade paperback.*

LILLY, ALTA.

by Kenneth Dyba

Two lovers, attempting to free themselves from the ruling matriarch of Lilly, Alta., unleash a chain of events which forever alters the small town.

2:55

BEN

It was so hot. Hottest I ever remember it ever being. And rainin' all the time. It'd been rainin' straight for a week. A week. Hot rain. Just like Moses Drumheller said it would. And everybody said for sure it was gonna wash away the polio. Gypsy kept sayin' it was a river from the sky to clean the town. Didn't seem to do much good on that count.

Constance Stebbings got it. Remember how she used to be around town everywhere, Willy? Everywhere you looked, there she was. Look at her now, Willy.

Otis and Otto Finnegan were havin' a field day. They couldn't get the coffins in from Calgary fast enough. I never seen Otis and Otto filled with so much life as when they were knee-deep in all that rain and dyin'. The rain let up some that one day and we all started breathin' easy. Everything seemed okay. Nobody more got sick. There was a lot of mess in town. But nobody more got sick.

Mrs. Edwards and Reverend Stebbings, they put together a clean-up crew and Mama and Papa, they join up to help out some of the Indians who were hit hard. Papa asks me to be a big boy and look after the drugstore while they're out in Indian Grove.

Mrs. Edwards and Reverend Stebbings, they pick Mama and Papa up in Mrs. Edwards' Chev and they all head out to the reserve just when it starts in rainin' again. Hot rainin'. Steam pourin' up from the roads. I'm watchin' from the drugstore window ...

Suddenly—I get real scared.

I don't want Mama and Papa to go to the Indians.

I go runnin' out into the rain, I hear someone yellin' that it's rainin' harder, even harder than before. Steam's boilin' off of me. I start runnin' over to Gypsy's. Indians're ridin' into town from all directions at once like they was being chased by somethin'.

"GYPSY! ... GYPSY!"

Right away, Gypsy grabs me from behind and throws me over to that big odd boy she had then and we're all runnin'. I'm being dragged, slidin' in the hot mud, fingers diggin' into my neck. Dragged, I'm being dragged by Gypsy and her boy up Boone Hill and I can hear people yellin' about the Little Lilly floodin' her banks.

And then everything goes black and it's like I'm tryin' to run under water.

When I come to I'm in that big reception room in Mrs. Lilly's house. That cougar head Quenten Boone shot at Crimson Lake, it's starin' down at me from the wall. And it's like the whole town's packed in there on top of the hill. Gypsy's holdin' me and Honey's tryin' to pour somethin' hot and sweet down my throat.

And everyone's standin' there, just standin' still as owls, lookin', just lookin' at me like I was in a coffin or somethin'. Nobody says nothin' to me. Nobody's talkin' at all, 'cept Reverend Stebbings who's showin' off prayin' with Mrs. Edwards in a corner.

Mrs. Lilly, she comes into the room and everybody tries to move back but there's too many people packed in there. That skinny Chas Halpern's right behind Mrs. Lilly like her shadow.

I could hear Mrs. Lilly tellin' Chas Halpern he might as well move in and run the drugstore now. Papa was drowned helpin' the Indians and Mama had to go to the hospital in Calgary. She had the polio for sure. She wouldn't last long for sure.

Calla was there, Willy, and she was lookin' like she wishes she got drowned, too.

After the rain finally stopped and everythin' got cleaned up, I moved our stuff out of the drugstore and stayed with Gypsy until you could get home for the funeral. Gypsy took me to Quenten Boone's grave to clean it up from the flood. Gypsy cleaned up Quenten Boone's grave. Mrs. Lilly didn't.

Gypsy told me Mama and Papa were her best friends in Canada and they always worked hard. For what, Willy? To help the Indians? To make Mrs. Lilly rich? To make Otis and Otto jump for joy? For what, Willy?

———————

Published by Playwrights Canada Press—trade paperback.

No crashers will be seen, thank you.

SERPENT KILLS

Blake Brooker & Jim Millan

In the mid 1970's a sinister gang of international felons crisscrosses South East Asia preying on young Western tourists. Led by smooth confidence man, Charles Sobhraj, and his Quebecoise lover, Marie Andrée LeClerc, the group was the nexus for a complicated web of criminal actions ending with the death of at least 12 young travellers.

1:55

CHARLES

(*on the streets of Singapore*) Observe Ajay. What do you see? (*pausing*) Any details? (*small pause*) Exactly. It's clean. The power of observation is one of our most important weapons. In addition to what? Psychology. Pharmacology. The martial arts ... and gemology. Guns are for stupid people, smart people use psychology. Singapore. The new face of Asia. Think of what you don't see. What's behind the smile? A clean street only means that litter is somewhere else, that the filth is washed into a river or dropped where no one dares complain. A city renowned for its cleanliness, shopping and lack of crime. Why is this? As there are many names for love, there are many names for crime. One of these is progress, another business. I believe you're in line for a promotion Ajay.

But we have to work on your wardrobe. Dress like the Boss, be treated like the Boss. In a cockfight, the loser is the bloodiest one. Or the one that gives up first. The winner never gives up and cleans his feathers over the corpse of his enemy. Exhausted he may die in the middle of the night, heart wrecked from effort but at least he's in his own bed and no one profits from it except his children. My father thought that France and Viet Nam was like a cockfight. France after sufficient feasting on our bones, went home with its red, white and blue plumes intact. Now France falls in upon itself, crushed by its own weight. And the skeleton of Viet Nam rises to victory over a confused America.

(*pausing*)No, we are not like Viet Nam. I am like the boy who cleans up the ring before every fight. The gamblers see a clean ring and the cock they've bet on. I see a ring that looks clean but I know where the bloody feathers have been dumped. Some people believe me when I tell them I've studied at the Sorbonne.

Available from Playwrights Union of Canada as a copyscript.

THE LAST BUS

by Raymond Storey

The death of a childhood friend brings Robert back to his home town where he forms an uneasy relationship with his dead friend's outcast girlfriend. Together they try to come to terms with past, present and future. Here he talks to his dead friend.

1:50

ROBERT

You were standing on the other side of the highway. There was a picnic or a field-day or something, I was trying to hold on to my mom. I was hot. She was wearing shorts and stepping on me. Tripping over me. She didn't want a mamma's boy underfoot. Didn't look good. When they said that there was going to be a race for boys my age and prizes, I didn't want to. I was the shortest and I knew I'd lose. I'm running across this field. It's rough and bumpy and sometimes there's rocks and the other boys are away, away ahead of me. And I know I can't win. And I can't keep running, so I throw myself on the ground. Everybody came over. They all thought I was hurt, because I was crying. So I figured I better pretend that I was. They gave me a rubber man on a tractor so that I would feel better. I could see in the set of Mom's face that she knew I was faking and she said, "Come on. I'll take you home." And I started crying and limping more so that she would know that I really was hurt. And the other kids and mothers were following us, saying is he okay? And my mom is getting red in the face and yanking me by the arm. Yanking me forward, not looking at me, and I hated her. And I hated those other kids. Pressing. And those other mothers. My mom's yanking me by the one hand and I got this stupid green-rubber man on a green-rubber tractor in the other hand and I just wanted to fold into myself until no one could see me anymore. And then she let me go. Everybody let go of me. They forgot about the falling-down kid with the green-rubber tractor and they went to the edge of the highway. Because somebody yelled that a little boy had gone across. People were yelling. Get back here where you belong. And I saw you. Marty. Hair like corn silk. Trucks barrelling past you. Yanking the air, pulling at your hair and your clothes, almost tugging you along with them. And you looked at me and smiled, like as if to say, "I've done it once, we can do it again. You and me." You were looking at me. Why did you do that? Why did you pick the falling-down kid with the green-rubber tractor? Why did you take him in, just to shove him out again? Why did you hold us here?

Published in Canadian Theatre Review, Summer 1987.

TODAY WE TEST THE TEACHERS

by Larry Zacharko

*We see what's learned but not taught in the education pro-
fession. What follows is a true story as told to the playwright by a teacher.*

2:00

CHRIS

I had twenty-five my first year. Twenty-four. No, twenty-five, but I
lost one ... Usually, when you say you lost one or when a teacher
says they lost one anyway, it means that the student transferred
away ... but this boy ... had leukemia.

I wasn't really close to him—I mean he was in my class and I didn't
ignore him or anything ... I guess there were just some other
students that I was closer to. Maybe because I knew he was sick
right at the beginning of the year. Maybe because he missed a lot of
school. He knew he had it and so did all of his grade-two classmates
...

It was ... the day before Valentine's Day. Valentine's Day was on a
Tuesday. He wasn't in class on Friday, but that was normal. He'd
look just as normal as everyone one day, then be in the hospital for
two, then bounce right back and be here for the last day of the week.
Only this Monday he didn't come in. His father did. His father
wanted to pick up the Valentines everyone had made for him. Well,
we all were working on Valentines and everyone in the class was
giving everyone else a heart or a Cupid that we'd cut out during the
last weeks. I said not everyone had finished—I had four real slow
ones—and I wanted to make sure every one of the cards got to him.
I was going to get some work together for him so he'd have
something to do in the hospital ... but when I turned back to his
father, his father was crying like he couldn't stop. Then he did long
enough to say "He's not coming back."

I didn't have all the Valentines; I wanted everyone to get theirs to
him. So I told him to come back tomorrow.

He died that night.

The next day was Valentine's Day. The kids were all excited because we'd planned this party for weeks. We were going to spend the morning finishing up the cards and decorations and in the afternoon we were going to have pop and popcorn and cinnamon hearts. The Principal came to my room just after recess and told me he'd had a call from the boy's father. I didn't know whether I should tell the class, but I couldn't do anything else; I was a bit shocked myself, I guess.

Some of the kids asked if that meant they weren't going to have a party later. Most were torn between the party feeling and the feeling that something important was happening around them. Some kept on repeating that he wasn't gone; that he would be back next grade.

Available from Playwrights Union of Canada as a copyscript.

THE STAGE MANAGER'S NIGHTMARE

by Mark Leiren-Young

From a revue of comedy sketches entitled "Watchin."

1:20

HOUSE MANAGER

Hello, I'm your front-of-house manager and I really must apologize to you for the delay this evening. The show will be beginning shortly ... While we're waiting I may as well tell you a little about the work. As you probably know it's about a king whose wife is raped by two gentlemen—perhaps gentlemen isn't the word I'm looking for—who cut off both her hands and removed her tongue in order that she will not be able to identify them. Eventually, however, the husband discovers the ruffians' identity, bakes them into a pie and serves the boys to their parents. It's a tragedy. A Shakespearian tragedy. That means everybody dies. If it was a comedy everybody would get married, except for the villain. It's not a very good play actually, but I'm sure you'll enjoy it. After all, it is Shakespeare ... And while we're waiting I'll introduce you to some of the people involved in the show. Fred Jenkins, our lighting board operator. Susan Wong, who does our sound. I'd like to introduce you to the author, but he couldn't be with us this evening. That was a joke. You see, the author's dead. Died hundreds of years ago. That's why everybody does his play—no royalties.

Available from Playwrights Union of Canada as a copyscript.

LEARNING TO LIVE WITH PERSONAL GROWTH

by Arthur Milner

Jeff's relationship with his wife is going nowhere and his job has become more boring and more difficult, but then he makes two new friends who change his life forever.

1:25

JEFF

Whatever the problem was, I couldn't talk to Marla about it. Marla and I can talk. We have really good talks sometimes, we can talk for hours about a movie we've seen, or people we know. But Marla always wants to talk about our relationship, and I don't mind, it's not that, it's just—I don't feel like there's very much to say. Marla thought that was a problem. I didn't. I've talked to guys I know, and I've asked women about it and it just seems to be one of those constants about couples. Women want to talk about their relationship, men don't. Women think it's a problem that men don't want to talk. Every night, I'm sure there's a lot of guys out there saying, "I think it's alright. I don't see any serious problem." For me, the problem was something different, it was bigger than that. I remember hearing on the radio one time about a couple who were celebrating their sixtieth wedding anniversary. I started to sweat. I thought, Marla and I have been married for eight years. That leaves fifty-two more years. Is Marla going to want to talk about our relationship for another fifty-two years? I couldn't very well say to her, "I have this problem. I can't imagine us living together for another fifty-two years. Nothing personal." But the thing was, it wasn't personal. It wasn't Marla that depressed me. It was the image that depressed me. I felt stuck. I could see myself in fifty-two years, sitting in an Italian restaurant, spilling over the sides of the chair, and Marla asking me, did I really love her, or why I wasn't as excited about her birthday as I used to be.

Available from Playwrights Union of Canada as a copyscript.

KRISTALLNACHT

by Richard Epp

A buoyant drama of love and loyalty set in Southern Alberta against the background of teaming POW camps. A German soldier and a Canadian farm girl are brought together under circumstances which test their humanity and threaten their dreams.

2:30

FRITZ

You want to know me? Well, alright. Here, sit down. Get your notepad, too, why don't you, so you won't miss a thing. You will hate me when I tell you, but if that's what you want ...

Please, I owe it to you and I have to say it. I can't be hurt by the Gestapo because, as far as they are concerned, I am on their side.

I don't know. Since I was a boy it was drilled into me. I was told, and I believed, we were an ancient race dating from Neanderthal; that we had the oldest culture on earth; that we were a people chosen to lead. And that gave us special responsibilities. In 1938 we were organized into groups of twenty or thirty boys—Hitler Jugend. A member of the Reich's embassy in Paris had been assassinated by a young Polish Jew, and the call was made from the top to retaliate. The Hitler Youth were asked to play some 'mischief' as they called it. We were to go into Jewish districts, smash up their businesses, set fire to their churches—a night of shattering glass we now remember as Kristallnacht. Several group leaders in our town organized their boys to take part. My own leader, and there must have been others like him, said if he caught us joining in he would personally discipline us. "After all," he said, "these are people we meet every day." Most of the boys went home, but not me and Peter Rechtsmeier. We stayed out just to watch. It was electric: the darkness, the flames, the sound of glass. We didn't watch for long before we too were caught up in the action. It wasn't mischief at all. It was savage destruction. And intensely satisfying. Our jaws were tight; we swung iron rods hard; we ran from shop to shop sweating, breathing heavily with enthusiasm for our work. And the glass fell like rain on Kristallnacht.

That was six years ago. One day in the camp Bruno interrogated me. It was frightening. He threatened to keep me off the farm. He said I must prove to him I was a good German, or else. And he meant business. I told him my story of Kristallnacht, but he wasn't interested. So, then I did a terrible thing. Really unforgivable. And it was so easily done. I betrayed my good friend, Karl Lehmann. To save my skin. And so I could work here and see you. I couldn't spend the rest of my life in that camp. I told him Lehmann had no confidence in the Party, which was true, after all.

I didn't tell him about you—your story, I mean. Though he probably knew. He knew everything. Imagine. I had informed on a friend, poisoned myself, and he called it worthless.

For me it was like Kristallnacht all over again. In six long years I had gone nowhere. In everything I had been through on three continents I learned nothing. Anyway, so now you can write your book.

Available from Playwrights Union of Canada as a copyscript.

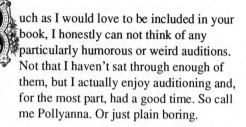uch as I would love to be included in your book, I honestly can not think of any particularly humorous or weird auditions. Not that I haven't sat through enough of them, but I actually enjoy auditioning and, for the most part, had a good time. So call me Pollyanna. Or just plain boring.

Michael Shamata
Artistic Director
Theatre New Brunswick
Fredericton
New Brunswick

WHO'S LOOKING AFTER THE ATLANTIC?

by Warren Graves

A comic encounter between a psychiatrist and a mildly insane millionaire of about 30.

1:25

CASEY BRANNIGAN

I have just finished Hobbes' *LEVIATHAN*. I didn't rush into it. Spent several days beforehand preparing myself, gathering my concentration, then I plunged ... A totally absorbing experience ... There are over six thousand "o's" in Hobbes *LEVIATHAN*. Next I shall tackle Plato's *REPUBLIC*. I have come to the conclusion that philosophy is a question of who has the most "o's." Whenever I have put forward an original philosophic thought, I have been greeted with such erudite answers as "Oh really?" and "Oh, I don't agree" and sometimes just "Oh?" If philosophy is just a question of who has the most "o's," it brings with it one clear advantage that has been hitherto absent in existential thought: it becomes measurable mathematically. Thus making philosophic evaluation available to the masses. Mr. Average, when confronted with such a concept as "The son is father to the Man" can riposte "Only two o's cocky" without giving the matter further contemplation. "So's your old man!" would be even better because as a concept in itself it contains three "o's" which is one more than "The son is the father to the Man" and three more than "Everything changes, everything is the same" which doesn't have any ...

Available from Playwrights Union of Canada as a copyscript.

SOFT PEDALLING

by Richard Greenblatt

Robert Goldblum, a rehearsal pianist fantasizes about life at the top of the music world. At the same time he must work out his relationship with his girlfriend, little realizing that his personal and professional dilemmas are one and the same.

2:30

ROBERT

Agh, I'm sorry. I'm not usually this ... feisty. It's just that things have been piling up lately. You don't mind if I use you as a sounding board, do you? (*laughing*) ... You want a list? (*rattling this off*) One: I've got no money to pay the rent, which is what I'm doing here, being a rehearsal robot, talking to a piano to keep myself from going crazy. Two: I've just parted company with the rock group that I was in for two years, over "artistic differences"—they wanted to go New Wave, and I didn't; and now they're getting their first big recording contract after all this time. Three: my younger brother just became a Born-Again Christian; and he was the bright one in the family. Four: my mother keeps bugging me about getting a real job, and I'm beginning to think she may have a point. Five: when I do get a real job, writing a commercial jingle for "Mellow Coffee," it gets rejected 'cause it's "too good." Six: I'm feeling old ... because Wayne Gretzky is just about the greatest hockey player in the galaxy at the grand old age of twenty; and, although he is a sweet kid, he finds it hard to string two words together and he's making a million bucks a year and I can't pay the rent. Aaaaand seven: the woman of my dreams ... wants to move in with me. No no no she really is the woman of my dreams, and I sure could use her share of the rent ... but ... I value my independent lifestyle and creative autonomy too much to exchange it for ... domestic bliss and ... and what's more, she's offered to support me as Composerman so that I don't have to come here, be a rehearsal robot and talk to a piano to keep myself from going crazy. All I have to do is say, "Y-y-y-ess" ... *(pausing)* Aghh, nothing makes sense anymore. *(as a hippy)* I mean, when I was growing up back in the sixties, man, things were clearer, you know what I mean? I mean, you knew who were the good guys and who were the bad guys back then. Like in Vietnam, man. I mean, who do you support in the Iran-Iraq war? Nothing's black and white anymore. *(as a TV commercial)* "You know you're getting old when you notice grey areas in your politics ... " I am getting old too ... man. Musically speaking, at the very least. "New Wave" ... "Punk" ... hmmm? ... You've never had a punk song played on you? You know, if we wanted to be real punkers, I mean, real anarchists, I'd just get up right now, right ... this ... second, and pound out a punk song on you. Can you see it? Hunh? Everybody'd think I'd gone nuts! Dancers ripping up their tights, and then attacking Frank with safety pins! The stage manager, for the first time in her life, at a total loss, while her assistant sets fire to the props! Aaaaand Frank, contorting in death throes from a thousand pin punctures, screaming, "That'th the energy I wath looking for! Now, oneth more—from the top! ! Aaaarrgghhhh! ! ! ! !"

Published by Playwrights Canada Press as a bound playscript.

She wants to see you. Ask her to come in.

MORS DRACULAE
(THE DEATH OF DRACULA)

by *Warren Graves*

Professor Van Helsing suspects the neighbouring European nobleman is responsible for the mysterious death of the young Lucy. He enlists the help of Dr. Seward and his sceptical daughter Mina to do final battle with the Count. Edward Renfield, an inmate of Seward's asylum, is under the Count's thrall.

1:10

RENFIELD

(*angrily reacting to the accusation*) No, I'm not mad. They think I'm mad. But I'm not mad. It's them. They are mad. They think they are clever. They are so busy being clever that they don't notice. Think of that! They don't notice that they are getting older. They don't notice that they are going to die. All alone. All alone because they are so clever and too busy to notice that people get old and die. But I noticed. I found the secret. You see the secret of life is life itself. Like the spiders and the flies—each one building upon the next and all part of the same. And you can live forever. The master will teach me to live forever. I shall never grow old. I shall never die. That's not mad. Only growing old and dying is mad. I can live forever. Like Lucy. (*noticing Lucy at a window*) She wants to see you. Ask her to come in. (*laughing and exiting*)

Available from Playwrights Union of Canada as a copyscript.

SLIDING FOR HOME

by Frank Moher

*Charlie Dempsey is a man with a dream, and nothing will
stand in his way—he must bring professional baseball to
"Edgmonton." He tries to persuade the president of the Pan
Pacific League that his town merits a "pro" team.*

2:10

DEMPSEY

If I could just ... describe for you my ... feelings for this game we
both ... care for. Y'see, my father was a fireman for the railroad,
eighteen years on the Albany and Schenectady Line. But his real
love was baseball, y'see, specifically the Buffalo Barons, and when
they were out of town and playing in Syracuse say, just down the
line a few miles, well he'd always have himself somehow assigned
into Syracuse. And he'd stay over, see, and watch the game. And
then he'd come home and sit by my bedside and tell me about it,
every pitch, every hit, every triple play in the ninth inning. So I
guess it kind of come to me natural. Now I knew I was never going
to make a ball-player. I could play first base good enough, but I
couldn't hit, y'see, that was my Achilles' tendon. But I could yell.
And I wanted to stay in the game, and I could see a play comin'
sometimes like it was written on holy tablets. So I became an
umpire. Northern League, Eastern League, California, oh that was a
good time. And when I was workin' the plate, with the players
spread out in front of me like a place settin' and the bleachers all in
a tizzy ... well, I knew that somebody wanted me there. I don't say
God mind you. But somebody. Although I do believe that God is a
baseball fan.

And then my Dad passed away, y'see. But sometimes, when I was
standin' there, I would hear a faint whispering in my ear. Just so.
Over the crackle of the peanut shells and the razzin' of the hecklers.
"I'm with you, Charlie. I'm here." And that, I knew, was my Dad.
Come down the line a few miles to see me work. "High and outside,

Charlie ... That one was good, Charlie ... Throw him out of the game Charlie, he doesn't deserve to play." Wherever I was, my Dad was there with me. So I had to stay in the game, y'see. It was the only way to keep him by.

And if I could just describe to you, sir, the scent of Edgmonton on an April evening, with the lilacs in bloom and the coyotes callin' to each other in the river valley! And the slap of horsehide just rousin' itself from the cold! And the way the ball travels, risin' to its apex till you think it can't go any higher, and then pickin' up the winds that come sluicin' down off the Rockies ... Well. Thank you for your time.

Published by Playwrights Canada Press—trade paperback.

VISITING HOURS

by Murray McRae

When Mother is confined to hospital for triple bypass surgery an antagonistic family is forced to reunite.

1:30

DAVID

Mom listen to me! I thought if people didn't know I used to be a doctor I wouldn't have to hear, "Gee how could you quit after working so hard and spending all that time and training?" I don't tell them over there. But I know. It won't let me forget. I was walking along Shaftesbury Avenue one day and a man was hit by a taxi. You know what I did? Nothing. I kept walking. Know why? Because I am not a doctor. I am a playwright.

Know what's funny ... that's what I was thinking as that man lay bleeding all over Shaftesbury Avenue. (*pausing*) It's not what I want but what I need. My needs versus his and I kept walking. Mom I need to write to survive. (*pausing*) It's the only way I can let what's inside of me out, all my feelings, my passion, or pain about things. I need to feel I am a success at something, and writing is what I believe I can succeed at. It's the only thing that matters. Happiness, whatever that is, seems to be irrelevant.

Mom, there is nowhere else I can go. (*pausing*) I don't have a life outside the confines of theatre. It's where I live, what I live on, and it terrifies me because I don't expect any more out of life than that. All the things normal people seem to strive for don't matter to me.

Marriage, a family, secure job, mortgage, a BMW. Once, they might have, but not now.

I wonder sometimes if it would've been different with Maureen. I wanted to marry her but she ... but, I guess she was just another casualty on Shaftesbury Avenue. I did love her.

Published in "New Works I" by Playwrights Canada Press—trade paperback.

MIDNIGHT MADNESS

by Dave Carley

It's the end of an era for Bloom's Furniture as its final sale draws to a close. Wesley has managed the Beds department for 10 years and his future looks bleak. Just before midnight, Anna enters his lonely domain and the course of their lives is changed forever.

1:25

WESLEY

You stormed out of here and never let me finish what I was trying to say. We were having a good time and then whammo, out you go, and I'm all alone (*snapping fingers*) just like that, I'm alone. You have any idea what that's like?

No. No you don't, you don't have a clue, it's easy for you to run out of here, you've got someplace to run to. You've got people, your Mom, Jason ... What have I got? I'll tell you what my life's like. When there's a symphony night I buy two tickets. I show up at the high school, they hand me my tickets and I shrug and say, "My friend's sick, I only need the one." So they won't know. I've only got one pillow on my bed—why would I ever expect a guest head? Some nights I lie there and look at the map I've got up on the wall beside my bed and I count all the dots that are cities and I wonder, "How many Wesleys are there in this goddamn country? How many others are lying there, alone, wondering what'd be like to have a real human being breathing beside them ..." In the winter I don't shovel the walk. Why would I? The only ones using it are me, the neighbours' kids flogging chocolate bars, Jehovah's Witnesses. Winter progresses, there's just this one deepening groove, one person wide, one neat path to my door that I follow up and down, up and down, until thaw ... one skinny little path ...

Published by Blizzard Publishing—trade paperback.

MELVILLE BOYS

by Norm Foster

*Owen and Lee Melville arrive at their uncle's lakeside
cabin for a weekend of beer and fishing but their plans are
thrown out of whack by the arrival of two sisters. The
women stay the night and become catalysts for a funny and
unsentimental look at four lives in transition.*

1:50

OWEN

Now, please, don't interrupt me. I've got all this laid out in my
head, and if you interrupt me, I'll lose my place. Now, I'm getting
married in three weeks. The invitations have gone out. We've been
measured for the suits. Everything's set to go. Except ... and here's
the problem ... Patty and I aren't right for each other. It's all wrong.
I can see that now. I was thinking about it last night, after you fell
asleep, and I said to myself, "Is Patty the girl that you want to spend
the rest of your life with?" And I thought about that ... The rest of
my life. Well, that's when it hit me. I mean, the answer is no. She's
not the girl. Oh, she's nice enough, sure. But, not for the rest of my
life. No, I realize that now. And it's because of you. Yeah, because
last night ... last night, I had more fun with you than I've ever had
with Patty. Ever.

(beat) I like you. I like you a lot. And I've got a real good job down
at the plant. A real secure job. I mean, I'm making more money
right now than my Dad ever made, and he was the foreman. And
I'm thinking of going back to school too ... Night School, so I'll
have something to fall back on just in case. Now, keeping all that in
mind, I was wondering if maybe you would ... well, if maybe you
and I could start seeing each other on a regular basis ... with the
thought that somewhere down the road, maybe in a year or so, if
everything goes all right ... maybe we could make it more regular.
Maybe even ... permanent. Do you understand what I'm saying so
far? I'm just asking you to go out with me for a while ... with the

option of marrying me later on. And I don't want to rush you, but I have to know today.

Well, I know it's kind of short notice, but I think I should call the wedding off, and I don't want to leave it 'til the last minute.

Did you want some time to think about it?

You're surprised aren't you?

(*laughing along*) Yeah, I figured you would be. (*the laughter dies down*) So what do you think?

Didn't you have a good time last night?

Published by Playwrights Canada Press—trade paperback.

'm sorry, I tried—I just can't think of anything worthy of publication. The second you go to print, a host of recollections will pour into my addled mind. Anyway, I just want as auditioner and auditionee to cry *bravo* to your project.

Graham Whitehead
Artistic Director
Mermaid Theatre
of Nova Scotia
Windsor, N.S.

Do you have something else perhaps?

ESCAPE ENTERTAINMENT

by Carol Bolt

A film producer, a critic and a movie star are marooned on the sound stage of a low budget movie in Kleinberg. Sparks and repartee fly.

1:55

PANCHO

Two years. Two years of PQMP's, then the CFDC, the CCA, p.r., c.p.a.'s BMW's and b.s. Do you know what I was like two years ago? I did not wear designer cowboy shirts for one thing. I did not owe the telephone company three thousand dollars. And I hadn't met you two years ago. And you hadn't stripped the transmission in my Trans Am.

And you hadn't stolen my heart. No, it's been worth it ... I think it's been worth it. I'm glad. I'm glad it happened. Because I've got your rushes. Because I've run your rushes maybe three hundred times. And every time I run that garbage footage, I get closer to it. Every time I watch my film go down the tubes, it gets clearer.

Because I see the light, Matt. I've seen the light, Matt. Look at that light. Look at that sky. It is slushy, isn't it? Don't tell me it will print up brighter. Don't tell me to throw more light on it. It looks like slush.

Do you know what happens in light like that? Not much. It isn't Carnival in Rio, that's for sure. It isn't springtime in Miami. We don't have bright white California sun. We can't put mariachi bands on Walmer Road. Incredible. You know what is credible in light like that? You know what I believe? There is some plot, some huge plot, I am at the centre of a gigantic plot. Some sinister, secret power wants a film—wants a very bad film—to use as a secret weapon. *Man with a Gun* will bore people to death and I'm responsible. Do you know how I feel in light like that? I feel responsible.

I feel despair, I feel self-doubt, I feel suspicion, paranoia ... But I also feel responsible, so there's a happy ending. There's a Canadian happy ending. Where my picture is a gross of guitar picks, but we learn something from it, we're all better people for it. I hate those films. I hate those slow sad films. I hate it when nobody wins. I hate it when the dream dies, when that's the message, that the dream dies. I hate it when it isn't possible. Whatever you want, it isn't possible.

Because it is. It's possible.

Available from Playwrights Union of Canada as a copyscript.

ZASTROZZI

by George Walker

*A revenge melodrama inspired by Shelley's novel in which
Zastrozzi, the Satan of Europe, engages in a never-ending
quest of retribution against his double, the saintly, deluded
Verezzi.*

2:15

ZASTROZZI

I am Zastrozzi. The master criminal of all Europe. This is not a
boast. It is information. I am to be feared for countless reasons. The
obvious ones of strength and skill with any weapon. The less
obvious ones because of the quality of my mind. It is superb. It
works in unique ways. And it is always working because I do not
sleep. I do not sleep because if I do I have nightmares and when you
have a mind like mine you have nightmares that could petrify the
devil. Sometimes because my mind is so powerful I even have
nightmares when I am awake and because my mind is so powerful I
am able to split my consciousness in two and observe myself having
my nightmare. This is not a trick. It is a phenomenon. I am having
one now. I have this one often. In it, I am what I am. The force of
darkness. The clear, sane voice of negative spirituality. Making
everyone answerable to the only constant truth I understand.
Mankind is weak. The world is ugly. The only way to save them
from each other is to destroy them both. In this nightmare I am
accomplishing this with great efficiency. I am destroying cities. I
am destroying countries. I am disturbing social patterns and
upsetting established cultures. I am causing people such
unspeakable misery that many of them are actually saving me the
trouble by doing away with themselves. And even better, I am
actually making them understand that this is in fact the way things
should proceed. I am at the height of my power. I am lucid, calm,
organized and energetic. Then it happens. A group of people come
out of the darkness with sickly smiles on their faces. They walk up
to me and tell me they have discovered my weakness, a flaw in my

power and that I am finished as a force to be reckoned with. Then one of them reaches out and tickles me affectionately under my chin. I am furious. I pick him up and crack his spine on my knee. Then throw him to the ground. He dies immediately. And after he dies he turns his head to me and says, "Misery loves chaos. And chaos loves company." I look at him and even though I know that the dead cannot speak let alone make sense I feel my brain turn to burning ashes and all my control runs out of my body like mud and I scream at him like a maniac, (*whispering*) "What does that mean?"

Published by Playwrights Canada Press—trade paperback.

I AM NOT A LEGEND

by Robert Knuckle & Gord Carruth

The scene takes place in July, 1959 in the auditorium of St.
Norbert's College, Depere, Wisconsin—the site of the Green
Bay Packers summer training camp. Vince Lombardi has
come to speak to his new team for the first time.

3:20

LOMBARDI

Good morning, Gentlemen! My name is Vince Lombardi. I want to
welcome you to our first day together as members of the Green Bay
Packers. It's nice to see everyone here so bright and early because
being on time is extremely important to me. (*yelling to coaches at*
the back of the house) You coaches back there lock those doors!
Nobody get's in here that's late.

Gentlemen, everything you need to know is posted on the bulletin
board in the residence. The only new wrinkle in the daily schedule
is that we're offering Mass in the chapel at 7:00 each morning—for
those so inclined. All the team rules are there but there are a couple
I want to mention. First of all, I don't like beards and I hate
moustaches—as a matter of fact I'm not that crazy about long
sideburns. So some of you people better get to a barber.

Secondly, don't ever go out on the practice field without having
your ankles taped or I'm going to have to fine you.

You'll get your playbooks at the end of this meeting. But you know,
rules and football plays are really not what I want to discuss this
morning. Gentlemen, by nature I'm not a negative person but we do
have a problem and I want to talk to you about it. Last year, you
people had the worst record in the forty-year history of this
franchise and that is a goddam shame—for you—because there's a

lot of talented people in this room. And you're probably very embarrassed about it all.

I think I'm right in assuming that you don't ever want that to happen again. Well then, we gotta change something.

Now I can stand up here and bullshit you to death for an hour or so and eventually lead up to what I want to say—but I'm going to come straight at you. I've been looking at last year's films till I'm blue in the face. And it was not your skills that were lacking at all. (*his anger begins to build*) It was your attitude! Over and over I saw mental errors and missed assignments. And what's worse I saw you giving in to fatigue and defeat when victory was right within your grasp. And so, I really have to wonder just how dedicated you are to this profession. As individuals, do you have the will to excel—to be the absolute best you can be at your position? As a team how resolute is your will to win—especially in the 4th quarter when things get down and dirty?

Dedication and will power, that's what we've got to work on. Those are the qualities that will turn us around and make us a winner. Without them you are wasting your time on a football field—or anywhere else for that matter.

Look at it this way. You are going to wake up every Monday morning, just as sore and stiff, whether you win or lose. Why the hell would anybody in their right mind go through all the pain and agony of a long football season if they're not going to end up being the winner ... simply for the lack of dedication.

Now, what makes it very easy for you to accept what I'm saying is that you have no choice, because if you don't dedicate yourself to this sport and this team, I won't keep you. No matter how fast or how big you are.

And the biggest mistake you can make is to leave this meeting and not believe that. So I repeat: Dedication, the will to excel, the will to win that's what is going to put a championship ring on this finger (*pointing to ring finger*) and on the hand of every man that's in this room. I promise you that.

Together, we're going to make that happen.

And there is one final thing. You've been assigned roommates on the basis of a shared interest—linemen with linemen, backs with backs—like that. Race or colour or ethnic origin was not a consideration in those assignments. And I have to tell you right now if I hear anyone using the words "nigger" or "dago" or "kike" or anything like that you're through with me. I will not tolerate that.

So ... I'll see you on the field at 10:30—with your ankles taped. Don't be late. Away you go.

———

Available from Playwrights Union of Canada as a copyscript.

DRAG QUEENS ON TRIAL

by Sky Gilbert

The Drag Queens each attempt to invent a colourful and romantic history for themselves, but when pressed, each must finally admit to a lonely past life and a future of ridicule, prejudice and danger.

1:10

LANA

And who are you, who is anyone to judge? Yes I am a drag queen and yes I am dying of AIDS. Perhaps I have made choices many would not agree with but I followed my heart and did the best I could with my life. For after all I have vowed to live dangerously and it has not been an easy vow to take. The life of a homosexual is by nature dangerous, we have always been laughed at, derided, persecuted, hounded, arrested, beaten, maimed, killed and why? Because we dared to be ourselves. Because we dared to live on the edge, to do those things that other people might be frightened to do, and so often secretly wish to do. Why do you think so many gay men have become famous writers, artists, crusaders? Because a passion to dare to be different, to live dangerously is the most enthralling disease in the world. And it's catching. Because when you have the disease you experience no pain. Because the real pain, the real disease is not being true to what's inside, is in being afraid to be afraid. I have not been afraid to look inside myself, to live on the edge of morality, society, of the world itself and if I must die for it, so be it. And to all the little boys out there who don't want to wear their little blue booties but pick out the pink ones, to all the little girls who would rather wear army boots than spike heels, to anyone who has ever challenged authority because they lived by their own lights I say don't turn back. Don't give up. It was worth it.

Available from Playwrights Union of Canada as a copyscript.

BILLY BISHOP GOES TO WAR

by John Gray & Eric Peterson

The truth about war. Billy is a high-flying ace of a show celebrating the derring-do of Canada's greatest pilot hero; Billy is an anti-hero. The Bishop myth is inflated and deflated in the same gesture.

1:40

BISHOP

It was a grim situation. But we didn't know how grim it could get until we saw the RE–7 ... the Reconnaissance Experimental Number Seven. Our new plane. What you saw was this mound of cables and wires, with a thousand pounds of equipment hanging off it. Four machine guns, a five-hundred-pound bomb, for God's sake. Reconnaissance equipment, cameras ... Roger Neville—that's my pilot—he and I are ordered into the thing to take it up. Of course, it doesn't get off the ground. Anyone could see that. We thought, fine, good riddance. But the officers go into a huddle.

(imitating the officers) Mmmmum? What do you think we should do? Take the bomb off? Take the bomb off!

So we take the bomb off and try it again. This time, the thing sort of flops down the runway like a crippled duck. Finally, by taking everything off but one machine gun, the thing sort of flopped itself into the air and chugged along. It was a pig! We were all scared stiff of it. So they put us on active duty ... as *bombers*! They gave us two bombs each, told us to fly over Hunland and drop them on somebody. But in order to accommodate for the weight of the bombs, they took our machine guns away!

(as if writing or reciting a letter) Dearest Margaret. We are dropping bombs on the enemy from unarmed machines. It is exciting work. It's hard to keep your confidence in a war when you don't have a gun. Somehow we get back in one piece and we start joking around and inspecting the machine for bullet and shrapnel damage. You're so thankful not to be dead. Then I go back to the barracks and lie

down. A kind of terrible loneliness comes over me. It's like waiting for the firing squad. It makes you want to cry, you feel so frightened and so alone. I think all of us who aren't dead think these things. Thinking of you constantly, I remain …

Published by Talon Books—trade paperback.

FIRE

by Paul Ledoux & David Young

The story of two brothers. Cale, the younger, forsakes his father's church to become a rock and roll star. He rises to the top but loses everything he ever valued, including his child bride Molly. Herchel becomes a minister and marries Molly but his jealousy of Cale drives him into the compromising world of TV evangelism. A Chalmers and Dora Mavor Moore Award winner.

2:25

HERCHEL

Friends, when I look about me today I see this once-proud nation of ours crumbling into the dust, and the reason that our nation is falling is that we are locking Jesus out of the highest offices in this land. You say to me, "Brother Blackwell, how did we get into this godless mess?" Well, you know what I think? I'll tell you what I think. I think that outside the fundamentalist church the people of this country have been deceived!

God help us, modern church theology has come to be based on a kind of dainty religious mush that's got more to do with John Lennon than it's got to do with St. John the Divine.

The Lord said: "Thou shalt not commit adultery." Modern churches are for teaching birth control in our schools and the rate of illegitimate birth has quadrupled over the last twenty years. That is a fact.

The Lord said, "Thou shalt not kill." Well, many of our modern churches are running abortion counselling centres in the basement. And that is also a fact.

Jesus said, in John, chapter 14, verse 6: "I am the Way and the Truth and the Life. No one comes to the Father except through me." "No one comes to the Father except through me." These modern churches are saying: "I am the way." The secular humanists who, God help us, are running this country are saying: "No, no, I am the way." Well, I am here to tell you that they are wrong! The modern churches are wrong! The government is wrong!

They're all wrong, 'cause I'll tell you, there is only one Truth, glory to God, and the Truth is in the Holy Bible! God's word: "I am the Way. I am the Truth! No one comes to the Father except through me!" That's what He told us in the book.

And if we're … if we're going to save this crumbling nation and save our souls then we need men in government who believe that, people. We've had enough of these men who say "I am the way. My will be done." We need men who say: "He is the Way. His—His will be done!"

It's simple enough. I think what we have to ask ourselves is this: "Are the men who are taking the will of the people to Washington Christian men? Will they serve the will of God in government?" If we ask that question of our candidates, and let the good Lord guide our consciences, then, praise Jesus, we're gonna turn this rottin' sinful world around. And if we don't? If we don't then as sure as this … (*holding up Bible*) is the Word of God. As sure as this is the living word of God, we are gonna burn in hellfire forever. You … think on that.

Published by Blizzard Publishing—trade paperback.

It must have been 1964. I'd been sent to audition for a cigarette commercial. The director pressed the ghetto blaster: "This is a kind of rock madrigal. Happy. You dance down the street and suddenly you see a couple in this cafe. They're smoking. You turn to the camera. You're very happy and continue dancing down the street." "I'm in the window, eh?" "What?" "I'm half of the couple in the window." "No. You're dancing." "Dancing!" "Dance round the table. Give us an idea what you do." "I'm not very good at that sort ..." "Come on. Come on. I'll fire up the tape." I needed the money to get out of the job in Simpson's Warehouse on Jarvis. The rock madrigal spewed out of the ghetto blaster. I danced round the table—or half way round. I had to stop. "Anything wrong?" The music stopped. The director, the clients, they all stared. "Sorry. Sorry." I picked up my bag. I fled. In the elevator I was ashamed. I sank down in the corner. The elevator stopped. I remember someone getting in. I got to my feet. I couldn't look anyone in the eye. I was ashamed. I went back to Simpson's.

There are very bad auditions. Better to go to ones where they let you talk, believe me.

Christopher Newton
Artistic Director
The Shaw Festival Theatre
Niagara-on-the-Lake,
Ontario

SCIENTIFIC AMERICANS

by John Mighton

The marriage of two scientists working for the Strategic Defence Initiative crumbles as the mundane and humorous aspects of their lives are contrasted with the monstrous strangeness and importance of their ideas. Bill is the military psychologist.

1:15

BILL

It's not easy working for the Department of Defense. It was easier at NBC. Here you have to keep track of every detail. You overlook one thing and you're finished. I spend most of my time writing profiles of scientists. But I still try to read the journals. I try to keep up with the work of my colleagues. Recently I learned about a discovery made in California: dreaming of revenge can improve your life. That's right. It's been proven. It helps to fantasize about getting even with people who've injured you. For instance—suppose someone cuts you off on the highway. You imagine his car on the side of the road with four flat tires. Or worse. It's simple. It's natural. You might try it the next time someone humiliates you. You'll live longer. Why don't you try it now? Go ahead. Close your eyes. Think of someone who's betrayed you, hurt you, stolen something from you. Form a picture of this person in your mind. Remember what they did to you. Now imagine a car. A 1985 Ford Pinto. On the skyway. At night, going sixty. Think about the truck in front of them. How big is it? What's it carrying? Is that snow you see? Imagine the flakes drifting down from heaven. Think of subatomic particles—the chaos that formed those perfect crystals. The truck slams on its brakes. Hold a mental picture of the person in this situation. Constantly hold this picture in your mind's eye.

Published by Playwrights Canada Press—trade paperback.

INDIAN

by George Ryga

A searing indictment of racist attitudes and practice against native Indians.

3:15

INDIAN

My brother was hungry ... an' he get job on farm of white bossman
to dig a well. Pay she is one dollar for every five feet down. My
brother dig twenty feet—two day hard work. He call up to
bossman—give me planks, for the blue clay she is getting wet! To
hell with what you see—bossman shout down the hole—just dig!
Pretty soon, the clay shift an' my brother is trapped to the shoulders.
He yell—pull me out! I can't move, an' the air, she is squeezed out
of me! But bossman on top—he is scared to go down in hole. He
leave to go to next farm, an' after that another farm, until he find
another Indian to send down hole. An' all the time from down there,
my brother yell at the sky. Jesus Christ—help me! White man leave
me here to die! But Jesus Christ not hear my brother, an' the water
she rise to his lips. Pretty soon, he put his head back until his hair
an' ears in slimy blue clay an' water. He no more hear himself
shout—but he shout all the same!

He see stars in the sky—lots of stars. A man see stars even in day
when he look up from hole in earth ...

Then Sam Cardinal come. Sam is a coward. But when he see my
brother there in well, an' the blue clay movin' around him like livin'
thing, he go down. Sam dig with his hands until he get rope around
my brother. Then he come up, an' he an' white bossman pull. My
brother no longer remember an' he not hear the angry crack of mud
an' water when they pull him free ...

My brother—you know what kind of life he had? He was not dead,
an' he was not alive. No. He was not alive. He was too near dead to
live. White bossman get rid of him quick. Here, says bossman—
here is three dollars pay. I dig twenty feet—I make four dollars, my

brother says. Bossman laugh. I take dollar for shovel you leave in the hole, he says. My brother come back to reserve, but he not go home. He live in my tent. At night, he wake up shouting, an' in daytime, he is like man who has no mind. He walk 'round, an' many times get lost in the bush, an' other Indian find him an' bring him back. He get very sick. For one month he lie in bed. Then he try to get up. But his legs an' arms are dried to the bone, like branches of dying tree.

One night, he say to me: go to other side of lake tomorrow, an' take my wife an' my son, Alphonse. Take good care of them. I won't live the night ... I reach out and touch him, for he talk like devil fire was on him. But his head and cheek is cold. You will live an' take care of your wife an' Alphonse yourself, I say to him. But my brother shake his head. He look at me and say—help me to die ...

I ... kill ... my ... brother! In my arms I hold him. He was so light, like small boy. I hold him ... rock 'im back and forward like this ... like mother rock us when we tiny kids. I rock 'im an' I cry ... I get my hands tight on his neck, an' I squeeze an' I squeeze. I know he dead, and I still squeeze an' cry, for everything is gone, and I am old man now ... only hunger an' hurt left now ...

I take off his shirt an' pants—I steal everything I can wear. Then I dig under tent, where ground is soft, and I bury my brother. After that, I go to other side of lake. When I tell my brother's wife what I done, she not say anything for long time. Then she look at me with eyes that never make tears again. Take Alphonse, she say ... I go to live with every man who have me, to forget him. Then she leave her shack, an' I alone with Alphonse ... I take Alphonse an' I come back. All Indians know what happen, but nobody say anything. Not to me ... not to you.

Published by Gage Publishing Co.—trade paperback.

JOHANNES REUCHLIN AND THE TALMUD

by Basya Hunter

Reuchlin was a 16th-century Christian scholar who opposed the Church's persecution of German Jews. He set forth to gain entrance to the secrets of the Talmud as a source of enlightenment to Christians at the risk of his own personal safety.

1:20

REUCHLIN

What is it you want of me? That I should tear the truth out of me and trample it under my feet? Why are we Christians? Why have we devoted our lives to learning? You remember our student nights, when we speculated endlessly upon our future? What careers we should carve out for ourselves? And it was you, Nicholas, who showed us the way. It was you who cleared our fuzzy student thinking. How well I remember your words, "It matters not how we earn our bread as long as it is by the truth." So now it is my turn to ask you, what has happened to that pledge you urged us all to make: that we never relinquish the everlasting quest? Nicholas, you do not fear what I have written. You fear what those who do not understand what I have written will do in their anger.

You are leaving? (*desperately*) Nicholas, you cannot leave. Not now. You are leaving me in sorrow.

(*suddenly exuberant*) We live in glorious times! An age of true enlightenment. Nicholas, you came in friendship, and that is suddenly so precious to me. Everything seems possible. I know you fear for me, you fear for the Church. But together we can drive away fear. With your help I can allay the suspicions of our colleagues. I can go wherever my Augenspiegel is read and teach what it is really saying. I will take page after page and prove that there is no vilification of the Church, that my Catholic faith is beyond question. And you will be with me Nicholas, I know you

will. You will help me to arrange the lectures. Together we will
pursue the truth.

Available from Playwrights Union of Canada as a copyscript.

BAD APPLES

by Michael Glassbourg

On the last day of school, the students in the "Rubber Room" have come to find out what questions will be on the exams. Unfortunately, the teacher is having a nervous breakdown.

3:45

TOMLINSON

Fifteen years I've been a teacher. From elementary school to high school, right into university and then, proudly, I became a teacher. I've happily gone from reformatory to prison to concentration camp to eternal damnation. I've sold my soul for forty thousand a year—not bad for babysitting.

Have you ever listened to the lyrics of Motley Crue or The Void? That's what your kids are listening to. Have you ever listened to those words? You should.

"Step on my face.
Kick my heart,
I need to know
you love me."

That's what they relate to. That's all they've got. That's what I have to deal with. I'm starting to see the sense of smashing my head against the wall, just like Sqwatch. I can't really blame him for making my life miserable. The superintendent is equally efficient ...

He can drop into my class at any time—and he does. One time ... one time, that sneak descended on me without any prior notice. Five minutes into the class, he was there. He sat at the back of the class, he didn't say a word, didn't introduce himself. The kids were looking around wondering what's going on, who is this guy. So, after a while, I said, "Perhaps, our guest would like to introduce himself," and he stood up and said, "Hi, I'm your friend." And smiled his weasel smile. So, Sqwatch stood up and bellowed,

"You're a fucking asshole." I thought my career would disappear, right there.

The people who ... the people? ... the guys, the men, because 90% of these guys are men ... these guys look, act like ... they have offices right out of Fortune magazine's fashion page. The one administrator I always have to deal with can never answer any of my questions. I ask him about a report which has his name on it—he asks his secretary about the report that she wrote for him. She did write it, but his name is on it.

She, not him ... she should be the one with Esquire's definitive desk for the power broker. She should be the one with the power. All he's got going for him is his gender and his ability to hire a secretary more capable than he is. What does he know about how the students feel?

But why bother with the students? The smart ones drop out anyways. What are they supposed to do? Sit here all day? At least I'm paid for the pleasure. I can afford an hour a week at the therapist. I can afford but I would never, ever go. Word gets around here quickly. "Uh, huh, Richard's seeing a shrink. Uh, huh. Uh, huh. The kids are getting to him. Uh, huh. Uh, huh. He cannot handle the pressure. Uh, huh. Uh, huh. Richard is frustrated with the system. Uh, huh. Uh, huh. Richard, we know a good vet. Uh, huh. Uh, huh." They'd think I was wingy. They'd think my curriculum is suffering. Well, it's not. I wanted to teach picking up candy wrappers and throwing them into trash cans but I knew they would never let me. It's terribly frustrating.

What do you do for a living, Richard Tomlinson?

I'm a stereotype.

Personally, I still feel I have my life in front of me. Statistically, I know it's more than half over—way more. But I still don't know what I want to be when I grow up or if one ever grows up.

Available from Playwrights Union of Canada as a copyscript.

WACOUSTA

by James Reaney

A dramatic retelling of the giant Wacousta's revenge on the British garrison at Detroit and Michilimackinac taken from the 1832 writings of Major John Richardson.

1:25

PONTIAC

I, Pontiac, was an opponent to the English ... these dogs dressed in red who came with their forts and their guns and their whiskey to rob us of our hunting grounds and drive away the game.

A message I received in a vision granted me from the Master of Life. "Lift the hatchet against the English and wipe them from the face of the earth." Serpents, harpies ... the English red coat hunting dogs have set eggs in our hunting grounds, eggs which they call forts ... nine serpent eggs. Fort Niagara, Sandusky, Venango, Presquile, Miami, St. Joseph, Schlosser, Michilimackinac ... Détroit. These nine eggs are filled with straight lines, free-ways, heartlessness, long knives, minuets, harpsichords, hoopskirts, death, disease, right-angled extermination.

One by one, under my leadership, we crushed their forts before they could sit on them long enough to hatch their murderous culture. Niagara, Sandusky, Venango, Presquile, Miami, St. Joseph, Schlosser ...

All save these two ... Michilimackinac (*pausing*) Détroit.

In forts, tough, hard-faced foreign devils, worshippers of the sky-demon Jehovah, shut their gates fast—hermetically sealed.

After twelve months they have divided my Ottawas from my allies the Potawatomies and the Delawares. With offers of a separate peace. Shall we think of peace too for a while? Shall we also smoke the white calumet with these foreign devils or shall we make one last lunge against these two remaining serpent eggs—Michilimackinac (*pausing*) Détroit. Who will speak for peace?

———

Available from Playwrights Union of Canada as a copyscript.

VILLAGE OF IDIOTS

by John Lazarus

*A year in the life of Chelm, the village of fools legendary in
Jewish folklore. Outsider Yosef falls in love with another
"stranger" and watches in fear as the "Chelmniks" prepare for a Cossack attack.*

3:00

SCHMENDRICK

I too have been a wanderer, you know. Originally, I hail from
Chelm. Not this Chelm: the other Chelm, the real Chelm. Living in
the real Chelm, you see, wasn't good enough for Schmendrick, oh
no. So one morning I got up before my wife and children—health
and joy to them, wherever they are now. And I started out for
Warsaw. To see the big city. In the middle of the afternoon, I got
sleepy, so I decided to take a nap by the roadside. But in case I
forgot which way I was going, I took off my boots and put them
beside the road—one pointing in the direction I was going, and one
in the direction I came from. After a while, I woke up, I stepped into
my boots, laced them up where they stood, and went on my way.
And wonder of wonders, I soon came to a village that looked—a
great deal like Chelm. And the closer I got, the more like Chelm it
looked! Tree for tree! House for house! Every blade of grass looked
familiar. You ever have that strange feeling that everything has
happened, just like this, a long time ago? Well, it was the strangest
thing. I walked down the streets as if in a dream. It was Chelm all
over again. The people I saw—each one looked exactly like
someone I knew back home in Chelm! There was a Rabbi like ours!
Here was a Zisyah, there a Mesholem! I turned up a lane just like
my lane. On it was a house that was board for board like my house:
even the paint was peeling in the same places. The chickens in the
yard had familiar feathers, reminiscent clucks. This was becoming
frightening. What if I walked in the door, and saw myself,
Schmendrick, sitting there in the kitchen? What would we say to
each other? So I hesitated on the front stoop—and out the door

came a woman who looked exactly like my wife, Shayna! Wart for wart! And she screamed at me, hitting notes I used to think only my own dear Shayna could reach! And the children were brat for brat like my own children—kvetching and snivelling and squabbling just like my own children! The only thing missing in this astonishing household was—Schmendrick. Their Schmendrick was nowhere to be seen. *He* had left *his* house and *his* Chelm that same morning!

I believe it was more than a coincidence: I believe that the hand of God was in this—or maybe the elbow, who understands these things—because, you see—the other Schmendrick never came back. And so, my friends—(*shrugging*) I moved in. At first I missed my own wife and children—but soon these children started calling me "Daddy." I guess I reminded them of their father. And soon this other Shayna—well, you don't want I should go into details. But I worry, you know. If the other Schmendrick ever comes home, it could get very complicated. But you know—my personal theory is that he wound up just like me. He arrived in my Chelm, and is presently living with my wife—the adulterous dog, may he contract the Czar's Disease—and worrying that I might some day return. And why don't I? A good question. To which my answer is, why should I? I am a practical man, Yosef. If this Chelm is exactly the same as the Chelm I come from, why should I walk my feet off to get to where I practically already am? The Talmud tells us that the world is everywhere the same, does it not? So maybe every village is exactly like this one, eh? Cow for cow, flower for flower? Who can say? Perhaps the entire world is simply one enormous Chelm. No?

Available from Playwrights Union of Canada as a copyscript.

TAMARA

by John Krizanc

A haunting portrait of fascist Italy and of Gabriele d'Annuzio, the poet and patriot who could have stopped Mussolini's rise to power. Dante is d'Annunzio's valet and an ex-gondolier.

1:55

DANTE

Emilia? Where is she? Emilia. I've spent six years in this house. This was my Venezia, a place where my mind could row back into time, back to Fridays in Mamma's kitchen, the scent of herbs and pastas, the smell of clean sweat, the sound of women working in the kitchen. Mamma showing Emilia how to make "challah," Caterina crawling on the counter ... Oh, Emilia, where is my daughter? I want my child. When Papa would come home, Mamma would light the shabbat candles and Papa would take Caterina in his arms and say, "May you be like Sarah, Rebecca, Rachel, and Leah." Emilia! Wasn't there joy then? Papa would recite the Kaddush and later he would read from the Torah and when I tried to talk you'd cut me off and insist that Papa continue. You were family, Emilia. And it could be that way again. It's not easy, it never is when you're poor. Mario says he fights for us, Finzi says he fights for us. They fight for power, power over us. If they don't kill each other, they'll end up like Il Comandante, old men who beat their servants because the world beat them. No longer. For too long I've said, "not yet." Not yet to my God, not yet to my people, not yet to freedom. I've stayed with Il Comandante because he took care of Mamma, because you stayed; no more, I am taking charge now. You look at Mario and think he is strong; what am I? Weak, afraid, and a fool? No. I may not be in the hills, but I'm fighting. Fighting for my wife and my child because a man's first responsibility is to his family. No more drinking or dreaming, or living in the past! I see this room and say; no more. This is not my house. The only thing left for us is tomorrow. Not next year in Jerusalem, but tomorrow. I will get

Mario out. Not for the revolution, but to save you and our daughter.
We'll get Mamma and go to Palestine. We'll be safe there. And
Finzi, if he fails as a fascist, maybe he'll learn to win as a Jew.

———

Published by Stoddart Publishing Co. Ltd.—trade paperback.

It was one of those long, uncomfortable cattle-call auditions that no one likes and I had just about come to the end of the day. I had heard a lot of mangled Shakespeare - "If this letter SPEED, my invention HOLD" - and there was just time for a few non-equity stragglers and then, blissfully, home.

A young actor took the stage, introduced himself and said he would use as his piece a letter written by Sacco on the eve of his execution, to his son. I knew of the Sacco - Venzetti case and was intrigued at this choice. It is a beautiful letter, but I had never heard it in audition. The young actor started. He spoke with conviction and clarity. He came to what I remembered was the end of the letter and I began to stand up and thank him. With the conviction that good material gives and the innocence of inexperience he looked at me with irritation and said sharply, "I haven't finished." He then proceeded to finish the post script to the letter, which I had completely forgotten about, and was indeed a most moving and necessary part of the speech. I hired him on the spot and wondered how many other, more experienced actors would have had the nerve to tell a director they didn't know that they hadn't finished - in effect, to take control of the audition and say "It's my time, listen to me on my terms."

Peter Moss
Artistic Director
Young People's Theatre
Toronto, Ontario

ANGLO

by Rod Hayward

In this musical farce about a unilingual man trying to fit into Quebec society an agent of the office de la Langue Française enters and views the audience suspiciously.

AGENT   *1:45*

(*taking out a paper and reading to the audience*) Mesdames et Messieurs. A public service message from the Office de la Langue Française. A warning to all Anglo persons that this play is not suitable material for a minority group. This play has an incorrect attitude. It fosters delusions of equality among Quebec anglophones. It may even cause blindness. Do you think a few cheap laughs worth the risk? For your sake, leave now. This is your last warning. Maybe, you got relatives in Chicoutimi? Or in Labrador? Cause once we separate, we gonna invade that there place. We gonna send all the Newfies back where they belong and make all those Eskimo guys speak French like they should. (*pausing*) Hey! You think you can just move to some other province, you? You ever hear of the O.L.A., Office de la Langue Acadienne? We're teaching those Acadian guys some good joual ... And what about that total immersion stuff in Calgary? And the French restaurants all over Toronto? You think that just happened? (*laughing*) Hey, we got you smart alec Anglos where we want you, all right! ... I guess you figure you're pretty safe cause you're American tourist person? In ten years, nobody be able to buy a sandwich in that Fort Lauderdale place if he don't speak joual. And we're gonna have a talk with those Creole guys down there and straighten them out too. Then, you won't think it so funny no more, eh? So listen to me. It's not too late to catch the end of a nice Michel Tremblay play over at the Quat' Sous. If you know what's good for you, you get out of here quick, calice!

Available from Playwrights Union of Canada as a copyscript.

NED AND JACK

by Sheldon Rosen

After his brilliant Broadway opening as Hamlet, actor John Barrymore climbs the fire escape for a late-night visit with playwright Edward Sheldon. The play captures both men at a moment when their personal and professional lives are faced with abrupt change. Winner, 1980 Canadian Authors' Association Award for Drama.

1:30

NED

Do you believe in the influence of the mind, Jack? The influence of the mind over the functions of the body? Do you think a man could willfully destroy his body?

I'm not talking about physical abuse ... half the time I'm not even certain I know what I'm talking about ... I mean, it's reached the point where, in my mind, I actually believe that in some insane, convoluted way, I have somehow contrived to bring this thing on myself. I admit it makes no sense in the normal way of thinking, but that's what I feel. In one way or another, we get what we deserve—granted, that notion may merely be the reflection of a passing mood—but what's so out of place here is that ... well, there is no question that I absolutely abhor what is happening to me—I hate it. And yet, as much as I want to scream at the thought of what lies ahead, it's going to be a relief as well, A chance, because of the uniqueness of my circumstance, to close that immense disparity between my inner beliefs and outer behaviour. I will only be able to respond in the purest fashion with people. No more conflicts of subtext in our behaviour ... a potential for something positive out of all of this. However, deeper even than that, and this truly terrifies me, there are times that I am as convinced as one can be, that I am actually and willfully doing this to myself; an act of will, perhaps even a subterranean act of the will, so deep that I can't even be certain that it's happening, but it is, and I am doing it as a punishment. Oh, there are reasons I can give myself as to why, and then instead of fighting that state of mind, I accept it because obviously I deserve it, but, I don't. Goddamnit, I can't possibly deserve this! My own personal version of mortifying the flesh to punish the body for crimes of the spirit.

––––––––

Published by Playwrights Canada Press—trade paperback.

THEY'RE ALL AFRAID

by Leonard Peterson

Frustrated, disillusioned, disappointed and isolated, Arnie concludes that he is so lonely because everyone around him is so afraid.

1:45

ARNIE

A wonderful night out, a bit chilly, but I like that at night. We're three blocks from the carline. I always take a streetcar to Eedlee's place, and a cab from there to make the money stretch.

And on the way I get entertained by Dad ... coming along in what Mom calls his usual state. (*echoing the singing celebrant*)

Those who don't dast
Seldom outlast
Guys who get smashed
And gals who are fast.
Drink to them?
Drink to them?
Drink to us
All!

Mom will give it to him, by not giving it to him. Sayin' nothin', I hide as he passes by.

Go get the spade,
Sharpen the blade,
Hats of the haid,
All good men are daid.
Drink to them?
Drink to them?
Drink to us
All!

Dad'll wanna talk if he sees me. Same old cabbage. How rotten the world is, and what a mess his generation's made of it: pickin' the

wrong fights, keepin' the wrong keepsakes, missin' what everybody
says you can't miss up ahead, the Future, and missing it. 'N if he had to
do it all over again, he's sure—yeah! yeah! And how it's up to us
young people, not to let'm break us, too. His war: a nothin' thing now,
where the conquered ended the conquerors. His brand-new-world
buddies: out for comfort and clout only for theirsel's. The unions they
made, (*pridefully*) 'at put a lotta bread on a lotta tables: (*regretfully*)
thinkin' still it's all bread. But I ain't in the mood for it: gonna,
anyways, be late, pickin' up Eedlee ...

Fools' cavalcade:
We've got it made.
God's taxes unpaid?
Come, join the parade!
Drink to them?
Drink to them?
Drink to us
All!

Poor Dad. Mom thinks he drinks 'cause he's wicked. It's not that at all.
He's burnt out, too many fights for lost causes. Licked! But some hot
ashes deep inside him won't 'low him to settle. An' comin'n goin', I
can't not pass the fence where he's scribbled with the dregs of a paint
can: Alf the Obscure. And who'n our neighbourhood doesn't know
who 'tis? I tried to blot it out a while back with a spray can, but it's
bled through. And it rides with me on the streetcar all the way to
Eedlee's: that auto-epitaph: Alf the Obscure.

———————

Published by The Book Society of Canada Ltd.—trade paperback.

BRINKMAN WANTS A JOB

by Greg Dunham

As the shadow of an eclipse falls on Prince Edward Island, an American entrepreneur and an Ottawa bureaucrat interview Islanders for jobs in an American weapons factory. Two families are torn between hope for a better future and their moral dilemma.

2:45

HE

I had a job once you know. I worked in the same office from the time I was 22 until I was 42. Twenty years of go, go, go. Knocking on all doors. Not waiting for opportunity. But, rather, going out to create it. I was a go-getter of the first order ... you may not think that about me now. But I had my eyes glued always to the next rung above me. Those below could look out for themselves. And then I was promoted to vice-president in charge of sales. Me. Vice-president in charge of sales. Here I was pulling in seven fifty a week, my own secretary, a company car, an expense account. Yeah, I was going places ... The very day I was to take over my new position, I went into the office as usual: Good morning Miss Lund ... I was everybody's pal, the greatest salesman in the world, been with the company twenty years ... And in one moment I saw myself retiring in another twenty three. I saw myself, alone and old at the top of a ladder to nowhere. Mister President. And I knew that no matter what else, I did not want to become that fearsome, wrinkled old man behind that glass door. I did not want to give over the rest of my life just to become that. I took the day off work. And the next. And the one after that. There were phone calls. They came from my secretary at first: I'm covering for you ... you're not sick are you? Then the president himself got on the line, buddy-buddy like: When's my latest vee pee going to make an appearance? These calls quickly turned to anger: I can't afford to pay good money if you're just going to sit at home, get your ass on down here or you're canned ...

I never went back. I went on a trip to Europe ... and then my money ran out. I played golf ... and then my club membership ran out. I watched TV ... but then it was re-possessed. Soon, it took no time at all, I was living in an empty house. Day after day I woke up on the floor and looked out of windows without curtains. Day after day the bills came in and I burned them in the fireplace. Day after day I looked at the bare white walls. The electricity was cut off, the heat was cut off and finally the bank decided it was time to foreclose ... Then one day the door opened and I met Aesop, the greatest friend I ever had. And Aesop said to me: Put on some clothes. I hadn't been bothering to get dressed for days. I took my coat and walked out the door. I hadn't been outside for weeks. The sunlight blinded me. I walked and walked and walked ... and later, I watched the For Sale sign go up on the house where I had lived. I watched the For Sale sign come down too. And later still I watched them move in. And sometimes late at night, after the dog has been taken in and all the lights are off inside the house, I crawl into the shed out back and sleep. It's not so sad. I got faith in exchange for all my loss. And that's just about the best thing you'll ever have. Don't really matter what the faith is in, so long as it's faith, it'll do. Not to be confused with belief, which is thinking. Faith is feeling. They can't ever take that away from you, that is if you don't want them to.

Available from Playwrights Union of Canada as a copyscript.

THE INVENTION OF POETRY

by Paul Quarrington

*Once upon a time Gary pitched in the Majors. He even has
a bubble-gum card to prove it. Moon was once nominated
for the Nobel Prize for Poetry but that was years ago. Now
they both live and drink in their hideout from the world—a
fleabag hotel. Tonight the plan is to stay sober and to create
a poem of beauty and a joy forever but writing poetry re-
quires a muse ...*

3:25

GARY

I started warming up. The county fair was set up, you know, beside
the park. The air was full of sounds and smells. Laughing. Hey, girl
in row three there smiling at me. Wearing a little halter-top. Just
smiling, nothing shy about it. I'm married, well, you got to
understand, I was a faithful husband and all, but after Melanie died,
there was sometimes when ...

All I'm saying is, I see row three smiling at me and I think, *all
right.* I start warming up. My arm gets good. I get comfortable.
Game starts. I got all my pitches working. Fastball. Curve. Sinker.
Change-up like an old lady walking to Church. Girl in row three
smiling at me. You know what I notice about her? She's cross-eyed.
Not enough to make her look dopey, her eyes are just a little bit
skewed. Well, you see a cross-eyed woman in your home park,
that's a fine and wonderful portent. Popeye says it means they're
watching the game in Heaven.

The Astros are falling like dead men. They're just looking at my
stuff. It's like they can't believe I'm doing it. It's like, what the fuck
happened to Kennelly? And that's what I'm thinking too, you know,
what in the world is going on? They go one, two, three. One, two,
three. One, two, three. Between innings I sit in the dugout. I'm
thinking, yeah, I got a hold of it this time. I ain't gonna let go.

She's still smiling, my man. Meanwhile, Fergie cracks a solo sometime in the fifth. I tell the boys, thank you, kindly, that's all I'll need. Seventh inning. I'm even faster. I'm shaving corners like the girls before bikini season. One, two, three. Eighth inning—I haven't even thought it yet.

The P-word. Don't even think it. So, the eighth inning. They start throwing pinch hitters at me. Monk Grabowski. He goes for a low ball, pops it up to shallow centre field. One, two, three. Between innings. I smile at row three. Don't think the P-word, just don't think it, Kennelly. Just feel comfortable. You finally belong on this motherfucking godforsaken sumbitching planet. Ninth inning. The word has spread through the fair grounds, you know, kid over the ballpark got himself a P-word game going on. People everywhere. That's all right. That's all right. I'm not nervous. Hello, row three. Shine up your headlights, sister, I'll be taking a long drive in just a while. One man to go. I think it. I think, Gary, my son, you got a perfect game going on.

Stupidest thing I ever did. So. Here he comes. He's big and ugly and he's got a potbelly full of beer and fried chicken. Alvis Rankin. Rank Old Uncle Al. He steps into the box. Smiles at me like it's a social event. The man don't know but one thing. He knows how to hit a baseball. I throw a fastball inside, try to back him off the plate. Ball screams by, cuts the corner, ump shoots his hand out, strike one. Rankin giggles. Until the day I die, I will not know why that man giggled. He stands his ground, too. So, next ball ... and this is the ironic bit ... next pitch is my mistake. It's soft and square and rolls over the plate like a Cadillac down Main street. But Rank Old Uncle Al swings over the ball, strike two. Now we start this old game, I toss 'em, Rankin fouls 'em off. Finally, I think, okay. This man intends to take my perfect game away. I will not allow it. I will throw my best pitch. It's gonna be fast and clean and lethal as grandma's twat. And that's the pitch I threw. I get goose-bumped thinking about that pitch. Only one little problem with it. Rankin took it downtown. Picked up the halter-top in row three on his way. And that was my imperfect game.

———

Published by Blizzard Publishing—trade paperback.

PAPERS

by Allan Stratton

*Two lonely and articulate academics struggle with their
mutual inability to communicate.*

1:30

CHARLES

For six years I have sat at that typewriter. I have stared at a blank
sheet of paper. And it has stared back. I have sat and sat and stared
and stared and nothing has happened. Nothing! Periodically, out of
desperation, I have ripped it out and replaced it with another. And
another. And another. And started again. And again. And again.
Staring at this blank sheet of paper. And it staring back. I sit and I
stare and I sit and I stare, listening to the radiator and the relentless
tick tick ticking of the clock, while the hours turn to weeks turn to
months turn to six years, my God, and me sitting in the dark staring
at a goddamn piece of paper that is driving me out of my mind! And
everyone asking, "What are you working on?" "How's it coming?"
And me saying anything to shut them up. Anything to make the
questions go away. But they don't. Every day they get louder. And
how do I tell them my voices have left me? How do I tell myself
that? That—my God—they may never come again. Writing is who I
am. If if don't write, what am I? And I sit and I sit and I sit trying to
forget the clock that tells me life is short, it's drifting away, it's
slipping away like water, I can't hold it, and every day is another
day gone and time is running out and I may never write again.

Published by Playwrights Canada Press—trade paperback.

MANDARIN ORANGES II

by Rex Deverell

A typical day in the Canadian Parliament. The house is very sparsely occupied. The speaker is nodding off. A single MP has obviously been droning on forever. He is reading— badly—from a prepared speech. As he speaks a few members drift in and out of the chamber.

1:15

MP

And so Mr. Speaker, I shall not take any more of the House's time on this matter—but before the Bill—Bill *(refers to notes)* 146: An Act to Regulate Poultry—goes to second reading, Mr. Speaker, I thought that it was—well, incumbent upon me to make a few remarks about eggs and egg marketing worldwide, price-wise. I'm not sure if the house, Mr. Speaker, recognizes that there is not just one breed of chicken involved here— and I have a list forwarded me by the Chicken Breeders Rights Association—and I'll be happy to share it with the honorable members if any of them care to see it—and I think this impacts on the present economics of the industry in the recent past. And there are a lot of ways, Mr. Speaker, that producers are able to increase the laying rate of hens, some of which are—well, I won't list them but they too can be easily accessed through this other document here—where is it—here—put out by CBRA and called uh—A Good Lay. So, Mr. Speaker, I'm going to vote for it in first reading—because, I do think, Mr. Speaker, we have to move on this issue—and it is high time—we can't sit on it any longer—but just how the issue is going to roll deserves a lot more attention and in my opinion this bill is not anything to crow about yet. Thank you, Mr. Speaker.

Available from Playwrights Union of Canada as a copyscript.

SEVEN STORIES

by Morris Panych

A man is perched on the ledge of an apartment building preparing to plunge to his death. All about him, the building's inhabitants pop in and out of the their window, revealing snippets of their own incongruous lives. As he contemplates the meaninglessness of his existence, he is unexpectedly and suddenly set free.

3:05

MAN

You see—my faith in the days of the week has been seriously undermined. When I woke up this morning, I wasn't exactly sure what day it was. And for that brief moment—it was only a matter of seconds…I think it was seconds…I stood or I should say I "lay" on very shaky ground. After all, how could I act with assurity? How could I rise up and plunge headlong into Friday's world, if it was actually Saturday? And so I lay completely still for a moment, pondering this question. That's when I noticed my hands. I'd never noticed them before. How they moved with amazing dexterity. But this flexibility, this movement of hands, can never extend beyond the boundaries of its own flesh—can only reach as far as the fingertips and no further, much as the movement of time is restricted by the days of the week. So I got up and tried to erase these things from my mind. I tried to get dressed. But then I began to understand other things—for example the meaning of shoes. They were little prisons for my feet. Absolute definitions of space. I could run a million miles, in any direction, and still not escape them. And my hat—forming a firm idea around my head, as if to say, "Well, that's about the size of it." My mind could expand into infinite space, and still never change the shape of my head. I saw in the mirror a condemned man, serving a life sentence inside his body. Even the car I drove to work. My car. This thing. This instrument of liberation. It wasn't freedom. It was merely the idea of freedom, bound in metal. A kind of hope, but with a speed limit attached to it. Now I was traveling an unknown route along a familiar road. It led in exactly the direction I was going, but not by coincidence. The asphalt was not laying itself a path in front of me. I was merely following a pre-arranged course and then something happened, something that had never happened before. When I finally arrived in town at my usual space, it was taken. I was late for work you see and there was another car in my space. Someone had taken my space, you see. I sat in my car for a moment, not knowing where to go. Just staring straight ahead. And then, I put my car into gear and drove into it. Drove right into this other car. There didn't seem to be any other choice. No place else to go, you see.

So I put my car in reverse, backed up, and rammed into this car again. And then again, and again and again, until finally this other car, this intruder of my space was smashed up against the side of the building, like an accordion. So now I had my space back, and I parked. I got out of the car, and turned to head for my office. That's when I realized. It wasn't my space at all. Somehow I got completely turned around. This wasn't anywhere near where I work. I didn't know where I was. I hadn't any idea. I had always depended on the road which leads there. The way I've always believed that one thing leads to another. Then I saw this building. I thought I'd come up here to get a better perspective on my exact situation. And from here the view is quite clear. There are no spaces left, you see. I have no place to park my car.

Published by Talon Books—trade paperback.

A YARD OF DREAMS

by James DeFelice

John, in his late forties, is speaking to his wife Virginia and her sister Bessie. They are sitting at a table waiting for their son Skip who is returning to this small northern prairie town from a professional hockey camp. John lives vicariously through his son's successes.

2:30

JOHN

Must be his coming home. Thoughts about Skip are rushing out of me. Remember the teacher that came over from England? Skip had him in the seventh grade. Always wore a starched shirt and tie. And a striped suit. Imagine. Here. What was his name? Knox? George Knox. Never forget what happened to him. Knox tried to stop a hockey game at recess. Thought it was getting too rough. Charlie Benson caught a stick right across the mouth. Think he spit out a couple of teeth. Nothing to worry about. Charlie was a tough kid. And you're gonna lose your teeth sometime playing hockey. Might as well get it out of the way at twelve. What's the difference. I was watching the game. Giving Skip some pointers. Well, I thought Knox was going to faint right there. Starched shirt and all. There was blood on the snow. Blood all over anyone who got close to him. But that didn't hold Charlie back. Score was tied, you see. Skip and Charlie were in the corner fighting for the puck. Keep in mind, they're using a frozen horse turd. Knox has seen enough. He blows that funny whistle of his. But no one stops. Then he charges out on the ice. Leather shoes and all. Fell right on his arse. Three point landing. Kids are doubled over. Laughing right in his frost-bitten face. Knox got up. Was he mad. He picks up the puck. "That's it. Recess is over." Very stiff and British-like. What the hell he was doing here, I'll never know. He puts the puck in his back pocket and goes like a head waiter in a fancy restaurant back into the schoolhouse.

Skip told me the rest. It was a bitter cold day. Inside the schoolhouse, the Quebec heater was really pushing out the fire. After about twenty minutes, there was this awful smell in the room. Everyone knew where it was coming from. And if they didn't know someone told them. Lots of whispering in ears. Everyone knew except Knox. He sniffed a couple of times. He thought someone had … cut some cheese, you know?

Anyway, on the middle of reading some fancy poet, he stuck his right hand in his back pocket and came up with a fist full of … well by that time the horse turd had melted. Whole class was on the floor. Knox dismissed everyone. Then he went downstairs, where he slept. A couple of the guys looked in the window. Skip was right in front. Wouldn't miss it for anything. He never liked that guy. Kept him after school too many times. Made him miss important practices. Knox spent all day and night scrubbing those pants. Put them on the line. Near the outhouse. And they froze. Had to call off school for the next two days waiting for his pants to thaw out. Turned out that striped suit was the only clothes he owned.

Working here kinda got to him. Went back to England at the end of the year. Heard he cracked up. Too bad. But this place isn't for sissies.

Available from Playwrights Union of Canada as a copyscript.

THE THIRD ASCENT

by Frank Moher

Henry Stimson, idealist and U.S. Secretary of War, climbs Chief Mountain in northern Montana for the last time seeking absolution for his role in the bombing of Hiroshima. Winner, Sterling Award for Outstanding New Play.

1:40

STIMSON

Hiroshima was bombed on the morning of ... well, that is all history. You know all that. The death toll was rather higher than we expected. We had thought 20,000 people would die. 70,000 died in Hiroshima. 74,000 in Nagasaki.

That is not news to you. It was news to us then.

By dropping the atomic bomb, I believe we saved at least a million American lives. By dropping the bomb, we may also have saved a million Japanese lives. We also put an end to the fire raids which had already killed 100,000 people in Tokyo, and destroyed or irreparably damaged such centres of culture and history as Coventry, Berlin, London, Cologne. We put an end to the military blockade which was causing such hardship in Japan. We knew what we were doing. But there were circumstances. Circumstances which I very much fear history has obscured rather than made clearer.

There is an assumption that distance makes clearer the nature of an event or deed. But it is not so. Study a painting from the middle of the gallery floor and you will see its total effect, yes. But stand with your eyes inches from the canvas and you will begin to see the brush strokes, the draughtsmanship, the choices of brush and colour that passed through the artist's mind as he stood in that exact same spot. It is only close up that an event can be understood; distance in time or geography only seems to make the event simpler. That is why there was debate in Chicago, and doubt in Los Alamos, as to the rightness of what we were doing. That is why you sit there and wonder at our hard-heartedness. But it was not that simple. It was not that simple. That is what I want you to know.

———————

Published by Blizzard Publishing Ltd.—trade paperback.

DOC

by Sharon Pollock

Catherine returns home to visit her aging father, a doctor revered and honoured by his community. She confronts, through a series of flashbacks, her thwarted need for his love and her late mother's decline into alcoholism, finally realizing that it is time for a reconciliation with her father. Winner, Governor General's Literary Award for Drama, 1986.

2:30

EV

If you want to know about this crazy bastard—if you want to know about him—when I needed a friend at my back, in a fight, in a brawl? This silly son of a bitch in sartorial splendour has saved my ass more than once—and me his—I'm gonna tell you a story. Now listen—we used to drink at this hole in the wall, this waterin' hole for whores and medical students, eh? And we'd sit there and nurse a beer all night and chat it up with the whores who'd come driftin' in well after midnight, towards mornin' really, and this was in winter, freeze a Frenchman's balls off—and the whores would come in off the street for a beer and we'd sit there all talkin' and jokin' around. They were nice girls these whores, all come to Montreal from Three Rivers and Chicoutimi and a lotta places I never heard tell of, and couldn't pronounce. Our acquaintance was strictly a pub acquaintance, we students preferin' to spend our money on beer thus avoidin' a medical difficulty which intimacy with these girls would most likely entail. So, this night we're stragglin' home in the cold walkin' and talkin' to a bunch a these whores, and as we pass their house, they drop off there up the steps yellin' "Goo-night goo-night" ... Bout a block further on, someone says: "Where the hell's Oscar?" Christ, we all start yellin' "Where the hell's Oscar? Oscar! Oscar!" Searchin' in gutters, snowbanks and alleys, but the bugger's gone, disappeared! Suddenly it comes to me. Surer than hell he's so pissed he's just followed along behind the girls when they peeled off to go home, and he's back there inside the cat house. So back I go. Bang on the door. This giant of a woman, uglier than sin, opens it up. Inside is all this screamin' and cryin' and poundin' and I say: "Did a kinda skinny fella"—and she says: "Get that son of a bitch outa here!" "Where is he?" I say. "Upstairs, he's locked himself in one of the rooms with Janette! He's killin' her for Christ's sake!" She takes me up to the room, door locked, girl inside is screamin' bloody murder and I can hear Oscar makin' a kinda intent diabolical ahhhhin' and oohhhin' sound. "Oscar! Oscar! For Christ's sake, open up!" The girl's pleadin' with him to stop, beggin' him, chill your blood to the bone to hear her. And still that aaahhhhhin'! and ooohhhhhhhin'! Nothin' for it but I got to throw myself at the door till either it gives or my shoulder does. Finally. Boom! I'm in. I can see Oscar is not. He's got Janette tied to the bed, staked right out, naked and nude. He's straddlin' her but he's fully clothed, winter hat, scarf, boots and all, and he's wieldin' his blue anatomy pencil. He's drawin' all of her vital organs, he's outlinin' them on her skin with his blue anatomy pencil. He's got her kidneys and her lungs, her trachea and her liver all traced out. Takes four of us to pull him off—me and three massive brutes who've appeared. Janette is so upset they send her back to Rivière-du-Loup for two weeks to recover. Oscar has to turn pimp till he pays back the price of the door, and everyone swears it's the worst goddamn perversion and misuse of a whore ever witnessed in Montreal.

Published by Playwrights Canada Press—trade paperback.

Really, that won't be necessary. You've got the part.

FIRES IN THE NIGHT

by David S. Craig

The moving story of Fred and Cela Sloman, who, for thirty-nine years, taught children in Northern Ontario from a converted rail car.

1:05

FRED

I was just remembering it. Jimmy was about ten I think, and before we went down I said to him, "Jimmy, you can go on this trip, but I want you to ask questions; questions about anything you want." So he just nodded and off we went. Well I'd arranged for the kids to have a visit with the Mayor and at the appointed hour we were ushered into this enormous office, with high ceilings and Hizzoner sitting behind a huge oak desk. So my kids are standing there gaping and the Mayor says, "Do you have any questions about Toronto" thinking, of course, that they'd ask about the fire hall or Maple Leaf Gardens … Well quick as a wink Jimmy Waters' hand goes up and he says, "What'd'ya do with all the garbage?" Well my heart stopped. Because I knew if the Mayor laughed, or made any remark, there would be no more questions from Jimmy for a long, long time. But he didn't. He thought it was a wonderful question, a perceptive, intelligent and original question. In fact, he thought it was the best question he'd ever been asked as Mayor! And he picked up his telephone and ordered out his personal limousine, and Jimmy Waters, eyes wide as plates, was whisked off, sirens wailing and lights flashing, out to the City Dump. He came back from that trip two inches taller.

Available from Playwrights Union of Canada as a copyscript.

GONE THE BURNING SUN

Ken Mitchell

A compelling portrait of Dr. Norman Bethune, the brilliant medical man who devoted himself to saving the world in China, Spain and Montreal. Winner, Canadian Authors' Association Drama Award.

2:50

BETHUNE

Good morning, gentlemen! Welcome to the Montreal Royal Victoria Hospital, jewel in the crown of international Medico-Pulmonary surgery. Now—what does that mean to innocent young interns like yourselves? (*pausing*) You're absolutely right, son—sweet bugger-all! Because, in fact, it's no better than some waterfront abortion-den when you look at the statistics. Riddled with bureaucracy and rotten with incompetence. So don't look for a medical utopia—here or anywhere. The inefficiency will make you sweat. The hypocrisy will make you puke. More patients die in the Royal Vic from the cautious fumbling of old men than they do from T.B. in the slums of Verdun.

(*pausing*) Cynical? Not at all. Realistic. To expect better would only create disillusionment. And God knows, there are enough disillusioned doctors already. When I was given a second life—through radical pneumothorax—I left general practice and became a lung surgeon. One of the best, according to some. Oh, not these old fossils, of course. There are people here who accuse Bethune of killing his patients. Well, it's true. I do have a high mortality record. In fact, I operate on cases they're all terrified to admit into their offices—the hopeless dying!

(*angrily*) So to hell with them! If you want to be lung surgeons, you'll follow my technique—fast diagnosis—out there, in the reeking streets of Montreal—fast operation, fast treatment! Yes, they die on my operating table. But remember—Bethune gives them a sporting chance.

(*pulling a stethoscope from his pocket*) First demonstration this morning. Identify this object. (*pointing*) Right! I believe you have a future in medicine, son. Well, take a good look at the "stethoscope." The symbol of life—right? Wrong! This little device has killed more lung patients than all the cigarettes manufactured by Imperial Tobacco! My advice—wear it around your neck like a magic amulet. A bit of voodoo never hurt anyone. Remember—the doctor is the holy priest. But for results—stick to your X-ray machine. Five hundred percent more reliable. And when you're ready to work—these!

(*presenting a set of heavy rib shears, gleaming*) Rib shears. My proudest invention. Look dangerous, don't they? Well, they're not made for delicacy. They're made to cut through bone in one stroke—to collapse the lung—give it rest. We're dealing with an extreme disease, gentlemen—and it demands extreme remedies. Make no mistake. You will get blood on your hands. And other unpleasant organisms. You'll have to overcome some pet aversions, see them for what they are.

Well, I don't want to shock you—but you'll hear lots of shocking things about Norman Bethune. Playboy—alcoholic—eccentric. Now—I'm a red! Ha! But if I'm ever remembered for anything—it'll be the development of the artificial pneumothorax machine.

(*showing a poster or diagram of it*) A pump to collapse the lung. With this machine, I am able to maintain my patients' lives—as well as my own.

Consider these thoughts as you memorize your Latin. Tomorrow's lecture: Bedside Manners and Bigger Fees!

Published by Playwrights Canada Press—trade paperback.

PURE-LEN

by Philip Fine & Albert Nerenberg

After an unsuccessful suicide attempt in which he fell on his partner and killed him, Mr. Gerstein comes to the Shivah house to absolve himself in front of his partner's son.

2:20

MR. GERSTEIN

Lenny. Listen to me. Your father saved my life. I didn't succeed at killing myself. You know what that tells me to do now, eh? I have to keep on living. I have to stay on this earth because I'm not getting off it so easily. Your poor father. I loved that man to death. I love you. Lenny my heart is killing me. Your father and I had been arguing all day before all this. Mr. Fishman was keeping this from you and your mother but business was going down the toilet. There's no market for shag rugs in Montreal anymore. I said to him we've got to change. Change businesses, change cities. Something. He kept saying no. What? Did he think money was going to fall from the sky? No, I fell from the sky! Your poor father. What a loss. That morning some rugs came back. Rejected by Zellers, would you believe. That was it. I told your father I wanted to take my half of the money and set up a nice fruit-importing business. He turned beet-red and crushed his lunch bag. He said that this was all my fault. I had bought too many rugs. Too many reds and greens for Christmas. And if I couldn't save the business, it was me and not the business that was a failure. He's right. My wife can't stand me. My kids are ashamed of me. I saw no hope. Who was I fooling? I felt like a rotting cucumber and I just climbed up onto the roof. I was crying. Montreal was grey. The whole world was grey. I stepped to the edge and waited for an answer. At least a little tip from God. Nothing happened except that I knew I was jumping off and all I heard was your father's voice in my head screaming. He got to me Lenny. I stepped off the edge because what was the fucking point? I was falling and he turned and saw me. With his fist shaking at me. There was no turning back. I shit my pants right there in the sky. No time to be dainty. No more apologies. No more kibbitzing. I was a big fat nothing. All I had left was the power of gravity. And that crushed him. Worse than the lunch bag. I didn't want to kill him. Lenny I can't stay in this city. Take it. The business is yours. My half too. Do something with it.

I've gotta move. I've tried suicide. Now I'll try Toronto. It's yours Lenny. It's all yours. The whole factory. All the rugs. You've never showed much initiative but try. For your father's sake. He called you a bobohead but try and make something out of that business. Look you'll have ten thousand carpets. That's a very good start. I've gotta go Lenny and catch the Voyageur.

Available from Playwrights Union of Canada as a copyscript.

D'ARCY

by Sandra Dempsey

*Song, poetry and drama combine in this presentation of the
life of Thomas D'Arcy McGee, Father of Confederation and
Irish rebel, poet and journalist. The public and private man
is traced from his rebellious youth in Ireland to his assassi-
nation one dark night on the streets of Ottawa.*

1:30

D'ARCY

I was walking along Wellington Street the other day, on my way to
… now, where was it I was going? Ah, right. I was going off to …
No, that's not right. I wouldn't have been going along Wellington if
I'd been going there. Well, I was on Wellington Street, that I'm sure
of. I was just walking along, minding my own business—I do that
every now and again, you know, mind my own business. And just as
I was passing this lovely little bungalow, I could hear all sorts of
excitable noises coming from behind the house. Well, of course, this
got my curiosity going, so I stopped to have a listen.

I peered over the fence, but couldn't see a thing, so, despite the
ankle-deep mud, I ventured forth down the path at the side of the
house till I came to the back yard—at which point I rounded the
corner and promptly fell flat on my face.

So there I was, desperately trying to regain my composure, when all
of a sudden I noticed two men, standing, staring me in the face.
Well, one of them comes over to me and he says, "You're D'Arcy
McGee." With those comforting words, I picked myself up and
replied, "As a matter of fact, I am, sir. How kind of you to notice."
He then went on to inform me that, as this was part of my
constituency, it was my civic duty to resolve a certain dispute
between himself and his neighbour.

It seems the neighbour in question, a Frenchman, had just received
delivery of some garden fertilizer, and his neighbour, an

Englishman, didn't appreciate half of it sitting on his property. All the facts were before me now.

The Frenchman on the one side, the Englishman on the other, and the most enormous pile of fresh cow dung I've ever seen in my life between. The solution came to me like that. Move the manure.

Now I don't know if you can imagine what it must've been like for myself and the Frenchman to try to communicate using two different languages separately. But trying to tell him that he had to remove his fertilizer, well, I think I must've insulted him five times without getting it right. And he was trying desperate hard to tell me something, so I thought maybe we'd get further by acting it out.

But that sent the little Englishman to fits of giggling, so we had to stop. Finally I got myself a bit of paper and I sketched out a tiny series of detailed pictures, showing the relocation of the dung with two smiling stickmen on either side. And it was as simple as all that. It wasn't the language kept us from seeing eye-to-eye, it was the cow dung.

Published by Simon & Pierre Publishing Co. Ltd.—trade paperback.

he most candid audition experience I've had was provided by a casting agent from the United States who was in Toronto to cast a huge mini-series. There were hundreds of parts in this series and consequently hundreds of actors reading for the parts.

On the day of my appointment there were about 35 of us jammed into a small room, all waiting our turn; some being asked to wait and read again. One could sense a certain disquiet in the air.

After some time the casting agent emerged from the director's office and addressed the auditionees in a firm yet understanding tone: "Look," she said, "these characters have no past and no future; no mother and no father. Invent something. Welcome to television!" With that she swept back into the director's office taking my heart with her.

I auditioned for that series three other times but never got a part. Moral: when auditioning for television bring several "invented" characterizations along with you: the text seldom helps. Bonne chance!

Richard Monette

CECIL AND CLEOPAYTRA

by Daniel Libman

An aged, formerly renowned acting coach rekindles his interest in life when his day nurse becomes his next protegé. She is talented but untrained and not interested.

1:25

CECIL

NO KIDDING! BIG DEAL! NOW LISTEN TO ME! Listen to me. Listen Rosita. I am offering you my world. My secrets. And that costs. You make a decision. Everything or nothing. Of course it's scary. Of course it's dangerous. But you make a decision. Don't tell me the answer. If you decide to stay in this house you will work with me. You will learn what I am teaching. You will shed your little walls. Someday you can decide what's right and what's not, but you cannot say no to anything before you try it and understand it. Otherwise I am wasting my time, and so are you. Acting is a profession. Making art is a terrifying gift. It will strip you ragged and give you nothing but the impulse to do it better next time. I will understand if you feel unable, but I will be disappointed, because when I see you I see something special, something that only happens a few times in a teacher's life. I see the rare spirit of genius. You have the instinct, the drive, and the ability to commit to belief, to a point of the imagination, and thrill others with that vision. I may be wrong. I don't know. I guess I'll find out. (*pausing*) I'm going out now. I will be gone for a while. If you are here when I return, good. If not, well, it has been wonderful knowing you, and I will miss you. But you cannot stay here just as a nurse. It would burn me. I cannot watch what could have been fetching pills and cleaning toilets. So decide. But whatever you decide, this will be the last time we ever discuss it. Leave, or stay and work. Period.

Available from Playwrights Union of Canada as a copyscript.

THE DONNELLYS

by Peter Colley

*A gripping and dramatic compression of the tragedy sur-
rounding the ill-fated Donnelly family of Lucan, Ontario in
the late 1800's. Jim is the patriarch. Johannah is his wife.*

2:00

JIM

I know, Johannah. I guess we've both known it for a long time. I'm
too tired, Johannah. I'm getting old, and I'm too tired to fight, and
too tired to run. I've got a feeling deep in the pit of my stomach. It's
like there's a rat gnawing at my innards. They're in my dreams as
well. I find myself looking into the darkness, and all around there's
these eyes watching me. Everywhere ... everywhere I look.
Hundreds of fat, black rats ... whispering and chattering and
staring. Eyes full of hatred and teeth dripping with disease. You can
feel their hatred like hot spit burning your face. And all the little
bastards are waiting. Waiting for the right time. I get the same
feeling when I walk into town. I look into people's eyes and see the
same thing, Johannah ... I see the same goddamned thing! Christ!
You think I can't feel it? You think I don't know what you're all
thinking? Can't you see it? One by one they've stopped talking to
us. One by one they've stopped coming around. We've still got a
few good friends left. But how much longer, Johannah? How much
longer until they're all gone? They'd like to break us. They'd like to
see us grovel. But we won't ... we won't.

(writing or reading a letter) January 12th, 1880. Mr. Meredith:
Sir—On the 15th of last month, Pat Ryder's barns were burned. All
the vigilante committee at once pointed to my family as the ones
that done it. Ryder found out that all my boys were at a wedding
that night. He at once arrested me and my wife on suspicion. The
trial has been postponed four different times, and although we are
ready for trial at any time, they examined a lot of witnesses but
can't find anything against us. Ryder swore that we lived

neighbours to each other for thirty years and never had any difference, and had no reason for arresting us, only that we are blamed for everything. They are using us worse than mad dogs. They had the first trial in Lucan, and then adjourned to Granton simply to advertise us. I want you to handle the case on our behalf, and if there is any chance for damages, I want you to attack them at once, as they will never let us alone until some of them are made an example of. There is not the slightest cause for our arrest, and it seems hard to see a man and a woman over sixty years of age dragged around as laughing stocks. Yours truly, James Donnelly, Sr.

Published by Simon & Pierre Publishing Co. Ltd.—trade paperback.

TAG IN A GHOST TOWN

by Pat Langner

Tag sits alone in his rocking chair reminiscing about the days when there were more than the one current resident of the ghost town, and about how the population mysteriously declined.

1:05

TAG

I had this dog. (*pausing*) Big dog. Real short hair, kinda sandy in colour. One ear standin up and the other floppin wherever it felt like. On his back was the good part. He had all this loose skin, piles of it. When ya got him to stand on his hind legs, it looked just like his pants was fallin down. He'd walk around town with this sly look in his eyes and this sorta half grin on his puss—see, he humped everything. Weren't nothin too big or too small in the whole damn town. Nothin he wouldn't jump on fer a few pumps a the old pelvis. Everythin from hitchin posts ta preachers. Hell, he got horny standin in a gentle breeze and he'd always pick the dumbest times. (*pausing*) Like at my grandad's funeral. They'd just closed the lid on 'im. And the preacher's sayin the last words before they lower 'im inta the soil. Ma's placin pretty flowers around the gravesite and just ballin her eyes out. Then the preacher kinda stops fer a second, "Is there anything anyone else would like ta add?" Well, old Pel, that's what I called him, takes his cue like Buster Keaton, jumps on the side a that casket and is off ta the races. Gawdamn. I didn't stop laughin fer days. I could even hear old Grandad laughin at that one. Right through the dang coffin.

Available from Playwrights Union of Canada as a copyscript.

BAT MASTERSON'S LAST REGULAR JOB

by Bill Ballantyne

An aging hero of the Old West is offered a celebrity appearance at a second-rate boxing match. This, he naively hopes, will save his fading reputation. Here, he tries to impress young promoters.

1:20

BAT

I was there when the Murdoch Boys tore up the Tennessee bank. We were sittin' on the porch, havin' some tobacco. They came rumblin' in. One of 'em set up a Gattling gun right in the middle of the street. Everyone was screaming, people were scatterin'. I went and got my Remington long bore. I hid behind the watertrough. I fired for nearly seven hours till all of them were dead. I was at the border when the Valdera gang attacked. They attacked with burning pikes, stuck our animals, raped our women, burnt down the parish church. There was blood on the hills for seventeen miles. The casualties were over a thousand. President Roosevelt congratulated us by wire. He cited loyalty and bravery. The Mexican border was drawn up. The whole command was given ribbons. I'm the man who caught Morgan Earp and had him hung upside down. He had murdered eighteen people—one with a mountain hammer. When I caught Frank Loving I chopped off his legs and put a knife in his neck. I covered Tuscaloosa, I covered Arizona, I covered most of the Indian domains. I was called the "Man in Green." I was called "The Invincible Man." I was a hero to many people, a knight in shining armour, a protector and defender. I'm Bat Masterson, the Hero of the West, the gunfighter, the Indian fighter, the leader of the territory, the man who never backed down, the man you could turn to in a time of crisis, the man at the centre who carried the load. William Barclay "Bat" Masterson. Bat Masterson.

Published by Playwrights Canada Press—trade paperback.

GHOST HOUSE BLUES

by Robyn-Marie Butt

Stud is a seventy-year-old farmer put in a rest home against his will. Here he contemplates ways to escape, something he likes to talk big about. In the corner is a new resident to the home, Zero, a beautiful woman of his own age who, so far, has not talked at all.

1:15

STUD

There's a few ways you could do it, eh. I figger there's maybe three. One, the laundry. They stick all them bed-wetter's sheets in them big cloth bags an' pile 'em out back a the coat room fer the laundry people. Now that laundry guy, he's like me forty years younger: so much sex an' muscle he don't notice which end is up. You could get up at night, crawl in one a them bags, an' get out that way. But who wantsta walk away scot-free ta start a new life smellin' a some other old fart's piss? So then there's the town group. Pretenja wanta buy a tie, inform them ol' biddies an' their supervisory social activities faggot yer comin' along, an' go on out ta town. Go in a tie store, maybe even git the tie, then don't show back at the bus-stop till they give up an' leaveya behind. But who wantsta start a new life by gettin' left behind? Besides that mall's way the centre a timbuctoo. (*pausing*) An' then there's three. (*pausing*) Three. (*pausing*) Walkin' out. Yup. Just get up, walk ta the door, put on yer things, an' step on out. Jist step out. Jist—like that ... Done. (*defiantly*) Well this place could as well be the middle a the North Atlantic, couldn't it? It's a long ways ta swim, ain't it? Gotta getjer strength up fer it, don'tja? Jist takes time, is all. Jist need time ta get it together.

Available from Playwrights Union of Canada as a copyscript.

SEX, COLD CANS AND A COFFIN

by Chris Johnson

Two men, John and Albert, alternately support and battle each other as well as senility when they're not plotting escape from their old folks home. This play is sobering and moving yet filled with hilarity.

1:25

JOHN

God! Heavenly Father. Our Father who art. This is John. John Ellis. Remember me? No? I ... I'm the one who used to spit in the holy water at Saint Tristam's on Second Street. Now do you remember me? ... Yes, I thought you ... I mean Thee ... would. Actually, that's not what I came to talk to Thee about. What I really want to say is ... God, don't flush me to hell! I'm not a bad man, not really bad ... I guess Thee haven't heard from me in quite a while, eh God? Not since I came here. I used to read my Bible though. Real often. But then Albert here ... that's Albert ... (*pointing*) Albert here flushed it down the can because I ran over his foot with my wheelchair. I guess it's in hell now. But I guess Thee know more about that than I do. I guess. Clarence used to read my Bible to me. And hold my hand. But Albert flushed him down the can too. That's only his body over there in the coffin. That's why it stinks in here. The food's bad too. No taste. Just like sawdust. And the cans are cold. Albert hits me too. With his cane. And lies to nurse. And flushes my medicine down the can. I guess that's all I got to tell Thee God. Except please don't flush me to hell. I'm not a bad man. If you got to flush someone God, don't flush me. (*pointing his finger at Albert and screaming*) Flush him! Flush him!

———————

Available from Playwrights Union of Canada as a copyscript.

CIRCUS GOTHIC

by Jan Kudelka

A one-woman show based on Jan Kudelka's true experiences with the circus.

                                                                    2:30

ELEPHANT

Hmn
Hot
Humans
Humans
Milling about my kneecaps their frail bones sounding
boards for shrill voices. Their sounds bruise me.
Inside my hide is a cavern of silence.
Between my bones one sound reverberates for a century.
In the space between my footsteps empires rise and fall.

Sometimes we'll go truckin' by a huge expanse of water.
Water—I can smell it.
Clean through the metal and the dust.
So I'll let him know up there in the cab.
I'll stamp my foot.
Maybe give a little bellow.
Knock on the walls a bit if the feeling's strong
Now does he hear me.
First I'm a sick elephant.
Next I'm an ornery elephant.
And before you know it I'm an elephant who needs a trank.
Hell, all I want is a bath.
I haven't had one on this whole tour.
That's eight months now.
I tell you I have to work very hard to keep my spirits up.
I mean, you go try lifting two tons of canvas up and down twice a
day, for eight months without a bath.
Rain is no good cause it's a tease, instead of getting soaked I get

moist.

Not even a drenching downpour is the same as a good soak.

What I really want is to be drowned in Lake Ontario and floated out the St. Lawrence on a barge.

Waving to seagulls on my merry way.

Or towed on a tanker to Ceylon where I could sip cool jungle sludge from the murky pools of the Babar Ritz.

Maybe a monkey drop down from a palm and scratch this America from my pores.

With a hyacinth behind my ear I'd amble down tiger paths looking neither left nor right for traffic lights.

And if a man come by and say HAUL THIS LOG, I'd pick him up and drop him right on his head.

No man come by to pack me in some tinbox on rubber wheels.

The only rubber I wanna see is the one called tree.

To hell with the harness …

But again I am here and I feel so cold and hot and tired and dirty and it's likely I'll live to a hundred and thirty.

If I committed manslaughter they'd shoot me.

Pachyderm paranoia.

I like to keep my spirits up.

They fired the man who beat me.

Humans in groups are like locusts eating the wood off a pitch fork.

When they turmoil about my kneecaps like a living sea I close my eyes and doze, half asleep drifting boat on a sea of their bitsy bones.

Available from Playwrights Union of Canada as a copyscript.

CLASSICS OF LITERATURE

by Robyn-Marie Butt

Abandoned at the altar, Harri decided to bury herself in books. Can the bumbling Ralph save her? The housekeeper doesn't think so but then, she's a pessimist. Enter the horse.

2:10

HORSE

I was out with my trainer. I ran in a circle on a long red leash. This was nothing unusual. Then something happened. For the first time ever I began to notice, not my trainer—fixed and slightly bow-legged at the centre—but things nearer to me reeling by. Trees loomed like half-formed creatures and disappeared. Sky became a revolving bowl. Fences became speeding train tracks and flying birds—in our combined momentum—flashed past like meteors of feathers. A falling leaf became a spark. Sounds whirled to symphonic stew. I was Motion's intoxication, acted upon and rearranged by breath-taking momentum. Even my pasture had lost its certainty. Clover I formerly munched had lifted into blurred living carpet which, if I were to grab a mouthful, would disappear instantly into stasis. The entire world as I'd known it had rearranged, speeding into skeins of colour and sound. I felt drunk.

Suddenly these visions began jumping to the right. It was my trainer, jerking on my halter with all her might and bawling at me to halt. I laughed. Her tugs might have been those of sieve through water, her voice a mosquito during Beethoven's Ninth. Unimaginable rebellion ignited in me like a firework on Victoria Day. The feeling spread into my limbs. My flashing hooves turned to gold, my mane crackled up electrified by flight. Then my trainer swung her whip and things crashed into focus like a ten-car pile-up of vision. I stopped dead, felled by habit and by memories of sugar lumps.

A man was running towards us. He waved a ring-box in the air, shouting incoherently about mistaken romance. He was wearing a blue tuxedo with a corsage in the button-hole. The corsage looked edible. While he and my trainer melted into a less than ideal embrace, separated as they were by the pasture fence, I leaped the gate and bolted for town. My golden feet redoubled their drumming. The beat of my heart became furious counterpoint. Blood rushed through my ears like the whoosh of angel's wings. I turned into a driveway. A poem began repeating in my head. I bolted up a front veranda not pausing at the sight of the cleaning lady chain-smoking in a menacing coat. Coat and cleaning lady swept past and I arrived in your living room, dazed, these words humming insistently, magically, in my head: I think mice are rather nice.

And you see, those are the words to the very first poem you were taught in grade one. Those words were your introduction to literature.

Available from Playwrights Union of Canada as a copyscript.

You want ears. I'll grow ears.

PINOCCHIO

by Maurice Breslow

A musical account of Pinocchio's struggle against temptation and his efforts to become a real boy.

1:30

CRICKET

And down he went, to watch the ants, then beavers building a beaver dam, then the birds building a birdhouse, then snakes building a snake pit, and finally lions building a lions' den, when, I think it was somewhere in the den, he remembered his mission. So, off he flew again, and finally arrived at the sand called the strand, which is another way of saying he reached the beach. He looked up and down, but nowhere could he see his father. He was worried now, because a big, large storm was coming up, and the sea was very rough. Finally, looking out to sea, he thought he saw a small red sailboat bobbing up and down on the enormous waves. He peered out to sea, and sure enough, it was Geppetto. Pinocchio waved and shouted, and at last Geppetto saw him and laughed and stood and waved and shouted, too. But just then, up came a big wave, down went the boat, and back up came the big wave, but no boat. Pinocchio dove down, came up, dove down, came up, over and over, and finally had to give up. And worst of all, was that when he looked around, there was no land to be seen, either. He must have swum very far. So now he had to find land. He began swimming again, and swam for days and days, crying all the time for his lost father, and getting more and more exhausted. At last he spotted land far off, and swam towards it. In a day or so he reached the shore, and managed to land safely. Totally worn out, he slept for days and when he awoke at last, he explored the land he had landed on. He wandered for a long time, hoping to find the Blue Fairy, or anyone. Unfortunately, he found something else...

Available from Playwrights Union of Canada as a copyscript.

 friend once told me a story that his father had told him. His father was living in Russia before the Revolution, and he saw a play by some fellow named Chekhov in which this actor suddenly stepped out of character and yelled out to the audience "I'm not a landowner; I'm an actor and I haven't eaten in three days. And you people sit there on your fat asses while others are starving!" After the show, the inspector of police went to the dressing room and—personally—shot the actor. Dead. And my friend said to me, "That policeman would have made a good director."

PRAGUE
by John Krizanc

Published by Playwrights Canada Press—trade paperback.

But I haven't finished yet.

INDEX OF PLAYWRIGHTS

Thanks, we'll be in touch.

INDEX OF MONOLOGUES

THE EDITOR

Tony Hamill has been editing Canadian plays for publication at Playwrights Canada Press since 1988 while pursuing an acting career. After graduating from Carleton University with a Bachelor of Journalism and Political Science, he spent three years as a newspaper reporter and editor before taking the plunge and moving to New York City. There he studied acting and voice for four years at the Herbert Berghof Studio including one glorious year with Uta Hagen while also working with the Manhattan Rep. Co. He is a member of Canadian Actors' Equity Association and captain of his pub trivia team.

PUBLISHER INFORMATION

We'd like to recognize the kind permission granted by the following publishing houses to reprint monologues from plays they have published.

Act One Publishing
c/o Playwrights Union of Canada

Blizzard Publishing Ltd.
ISBN (0-921368) CIP
SAN 116-0575
301-89 Princess St.
Winnipeg, Man. R3B 1K6
Tel: (204) 949-0511
Fax: (204) 943-4129

Coach House Press
ISBN (0-88910) CIP
SAN 115-0251
401 (rear) Huron St.,
Toronto, Ont. M5S 2G5
Tel: (416) 979-7374
Fax: (416) 979-7006

Canadian Theatre Review
Available through subscription from:
Journals Department
University of Toronto Press
5201 Dufferin Street
Downsview, Ontario
M3H 5T8

Fifth House Publishers
ISBN (0-920079) CIP
SAN 115-141X
620 Duchess St.
Saskatoon, Sask. S7K 0R1
Tel: (306) 242-4936
Fax: (306) 242-7667
Order from University of Toronto Press

Gage Educational Publishing Company
A Division of Canada Publishing
Corporation
ISBN (0-7715, 0-7705) CIP
SAN 115-0375
164 Commander Blvd.
Agincourt, Ont. M1S 3C7
Telex: 065-25374
Tel: (416) 293-8141
Fax: (416) 293-9009

General Publishing Co. Ltd—*Orders:*
30 Lesmill Rd.
Don Mills, Ont., M3B 2T6
Tel: (416) 445-3333
Fax: (416) 445-5967

Lazara Publications
Box 2269
Vancouver Main Post Office
Vancouver, B.C.
V6B 3W2

NeWest Publishers Ltd.
10359 82nd Avenue, Suite 310
Edmonton, Alberta
T6E 1Z9
Tel: (403) 432-9427
Fax: (403) 431-0197

Playwrights Canada Press
Playwrights Union of Canada
ISBN (0-88754, 0-919834) CIP
SAN 115-0766
54 Wolseley St., 2nd Floor
Toronto, Ont. M5T 1A5
Tel: (416) 947-0201
Fax: (416) 947-0159

Porcepic Books
ISBN (0-88878) CIP
SAN 115-0812
4252 Commerce Crt.
Victoria, B.C. V8Z 4M2
Tel: (604) 727-6522
Fax: (604) 727-6418
Order desk: (800) 663-7560

Samuel French, Inc. —
Orders/Performance Requests to:

In the Eastern United States:
Samuel French, Inc.
45 W. 25th St.
New York, N.Y. 10010
Tel: (212) 206-8990
Fax: (212) 206-1429

In the Western United States:
Samuel French, Inc
7623 Sunset Blvd.
Hollywood, CA 90046
Tel: (213) 876-0570
Fax: (213) 876-6822

In Canada:
Samuel French, (Canada) Inc.
80 Richmond St. East
Toronto, Ont. M5C 1P1
Tel: (416) 363-3536 or 363-8417

Simon & Pierre Publishing
Company Ltd.
ISBN (0-88924) CIP
SAN 115-0952, 115-5229
Office and Warehouse:
815 Danforth Ave., Suite 404
Toronto, Ont. M4J 1L2
Tel: (416) 463-0313
Fax: (416) 463-4155
Order from University of Toronto Press

Stoddart Publishing Co. Limited
34 Lesmill Road
Toronto, Ont. M3B 2T6
Tel: (416) 445-3333
Fax: (416) 445-5967

Talon Books
ISBN (0-88922) CIP
SAN 115-5334
201 - 1019 East Cordova St.
Vancouver, B.C. V6A 1M8
Tel: (604) 253-5261
Fax: (604) 255-5755
Order from University of Toronto Press

University of Toronto Press—*Orders:*
5201 Dufferin St.
Downsview, Ont., M3H 5T8
Tel: (416) 667-7791/2/3/4
Fax: (416) 667-7832